THE KETOGENIC DIET FOR TYPE 1 DIABETES

Reduce Your HbA1c and Avoid Diabetic Complications

ELLEN DAVIS ◆ KEITH RUNYAN

Gutsy Badger Publishing

CHEYENNE, WYOMING

Ellen Davis
Gutsy Badger Publishing
Cheyenne, Wyoming
Email: ask.ellen.davis@gmail.com
Visit www.ketogenic-diet-resource.com

All of the information provided in and throughout this book (hereafter known as Publication) and offered at http://www.ketogenic-diet-resource.com is intended solely for general information and should NOT be relied upon for any particular diagnosis, treatment, or care. This is not a substitute for medical advice or treatment. This Publication and the website are only for general informational purposes. It is strongly encouraged that individuals and their families consult with qualified medical professionals for treatment and related advice on individual cases before beginning any diet. The full legal disclaimer is located in appendix E.

The Ketogenic Diet for Type 1 Diabetes / Ellen Davis and Keith Runyan

ISBN 978-1-943721-05-4 (Paperback)

ISBN 978-1-943721-07-8 (Electronic)

To everyone struggling with the harsh reality of a diabetes diagnosis and, especially, to my mother, who died of diabetic complications and liver cancer at the young age of sixty-three. I wish with all my heart that I had known then what I know now.

Ellen Davis, MS

To all who are affected every hour of every day with diabetes: to those concerned with when the next low-blood-sugar event will occur; to those worried about future complications of diabetes, including blindness, amputation, kidney failure, heart disease, and premature death; and to those who will need ever-increasing medications at ever-increasing costs on their current high-carbohydrate diets. The information presented here has given many of my patients (and me) a new lease on life. It is my sincere hope that you will experience all the benefits that my patients and I are now enjoying: reduction or elimination of hypoglycemia, hyperglycemia, and diabetic complications, along with an improvement in blood sugars and a reduction in medications.

And to my parents, Barbara Z. Runyan and John W. Runyan Jr., who have supported me my entire life and therefore made this book possible.

Keith R. Runyan, MS, MD

Contents

Using This Book

Here are some tips on getting the most out of this book.

- Do yourself a favor: Read this entire book carefully. Don't skim it or skip pages. Although we welcome questions, individuals have written to us about suffering side effects that could have been avoided by reading the book carefully and in its entirety.

- In the References section, we have included a glossary of terms and endnotes listing studies that support the statements in this book. The endnotes are designated throughout the book by number.

- Additional information and more technical discussions on various topics are discussed in separate Tech Notes, which are available at no charge upon request. These notes are supplemental information and are offered for those who appreciate learning more about the science and medicine of health and diabetes. If you are that type of person, please let us know, and we will email you a PDF of the information, or you can download the file from this link: http://www.ketogenic-diet-resource.com/support-files/kd-t1-diabetes-tn.pdf.

Introduction

This book is designed to introduce to you an underutilized but well-researched form of treatment for diabetes, the ketogenic diet. This is not a new "fad" diet. It was first devised by Dr. John Rollo in 1797. Clinical studies of its use were published in 1921, prior to the discovery of insulin that same year.[1] The discovery of insulin in 1921 was considered "the cure" for diabetes, and dietary changes were no longer promoted.

Our goal is to help you understand why current methods of diabetes treatment, which use a high-carbohydrate diet and insulin, are ineffective by comparison. The ketogenic diet, combined with insulin, is a powerful tool for normalizing blood sugar (blood glucose). This combination can minimize costly and disabling long-term complications of diabetes while simultaneously minimizing hypoglycemia (low blood sugar). As a bonus, following the diet can reduce insulin and medication requirements, which not only reduces the cost of caring for diabetes but also reduces the potential for side effects.

In working with your physician and learning how to manage diabetes with a ketogenic diet, you will be able to control your blood sugar more effectively with less insulin. In addition, your success in improving blood-sugar control and minimizing hypoglycemia may convince your physician to share this highly effective treatment with their other diabetic patients.

As with any diabetes treatment, the ketogenic diet needs to be combined with close monitoring of blood sugar. Urine and/or blood ketones may also require monitoring at times, and insulin dosages and other medications may need to be adjusted to maintain normal blood-glucose levels. Better blood-sugar control, fewer episodes of hypoglycemia, and a reduction in the complications of diabetes are the rewards for those who are willing to faithfully follow a ketogenic diet.

As a type 1 diabetic and a physician specializing in internal medicine, Dr. Runyan draws from both his personal experience and his clinical experience with the ketogenic diet in the treatment of diabetes in adults. He has personally witnessed many patients realize a drastic reduction in their insulin requirements after putting them on the diet.

We are aware that the ketogenic diet goes against conventional wisdom. Should you decide to adopt this lifestyle, you may receive cautionary warnings from your friends, your family, or even your doctor—warnings like "All that fat will clog your arteries," or "You need 130 grams of carbohydrate per day to fuel your brain," or "Your cholesterol will increase, and that's bad for your heart." You get the picture. We will attempt to dispel these and other myths regarding a ketogenic diet.

The stakes are high. Never underestimate the adverse consequences of elevated blood sugars and frequent or severe low blood sugars. Dr. Runyan has spent a career treating diabetic complications, including end-stage kidney failure as a result of diabetic nephropathy. He has also seen patients in a permanent comatose state from anoxic brain injury due to prolonged severe hypoglycemia. Equally sad, he knows of two young resident physicians with type 1 diabetes who died of hypoglycemia while on duty at the hospital. Thousands of people suffer tragic diabetic events in the United States each year[2]. Many of these events are avoidable if people have the knowledge and the will to carefully follow the suggestions contained in this book under their physician's supervision.

Finally, we acknowledge that the ketogenic diet is not necessarily the best nor the optimal diet for all people. If, after consultation with your physician or other professional advisors knowledgeable in the ketogenic diet, you are not realizing improvements or find that the ketogenic lifestyle is not enjoyable or otherwise not right for you, please adjust the diet or find another approach to treating your diabetes. Where there's a will, there's a way—you just need to find yours.

Preface

Hello and welcome! My name is Ellen Davis, and I thank you for your interest in this book. I am the author of Ketogenic Diet Resource, a website which showcases how a ketogenic diet can be used to improve many disease conditions, and in particular, all forms of diabetes. Utilizing a ketogenic diet can help those with diabetes control their blood sugar much more easily and effectively, which means they will be able to enjoy a much improved quality of life, and avoid the menace of diabetic complications in the future.

My coauthor, Dr. Keith Runyan, is a retired physician who has type 1 diabetes, so he has intimate knowledge about effective management of this disease. His personal story in chapter 1 is a powerful testament to the benefits that people with diabetes can expect when adopting a ketogenic diet.

Although I have a master of science degree in applied clinical nutrition and Dr. Runyan is a physician, we both recommend that your personal physician be involved in the review and application of information in this book. This dietary change has a powerful effect on the body, and insulin dosages will need to be reduced from the start of the diet. The same goes for other medications, such as those for lowering blood pressure.

I've learned over the years that each day offers a new opportunity for improved health, and it's never too late to take better care of yourself. I hope the information in this book will help you achieve that objective.

Ellen Davis, MS

Hello, my name is Keith Runyan, and I'm a retired physician who practiced internal medicine, nephrology, and obesity medicine in St. Petersburg, Florida. I attended medical school at Emory University School of Medicine in Atlanta, Georgia. Upon graduation from medical school in 1986, I completed my internship and residency in internal medicine at the Emory University Affiliated Hospitals Program. I decided to subspecialize in nephrology, which deals with the diagnosis and treatment of kidney diseases and the treatment of kidney failure with dialysis and kidney transplantation. I am board certified in internal medicine and nephrology by the American Board of Internal Medicine and in obesity medicine by the American Board of Obesity Medicine.

In 1998, I was diagnosed with type 1 diabetes, also called latent autoimmune diabetes in adults (LADA). I treated my diabetes as recommended by the American Diabetes Association (ADA). Although my HbA1c values (a measure of average blood sugar) were in the recommended range, they were not normal, which put me at risk for diabetic complications. In addition, I was having two to five low-blood-sugar episodes each week, which was both miserable and life-threatening. I found the solution to these problems: the ketogenic diet.

After adopting the diet in February 2012, I found that my hypoglycemia was markedly reduced and my blood-sugar control was much improved. I feel obligated to convey this information to others who are willing to receive it. This is the reason for writing this book. My coauthor, Ellen Davis, has a different story but found the same solution in the ketogenic diet, and we have teamed up as advocates for this lifestyle.

Keith Runyan, MS, MD

Part 1

Setting the Stage

1

Power of the Ketogenic Diet: Personal Stories

We think real results are of great interest to all. Here are a few accounts of people who have used a ketogenic diet to improve their type 1 or type 2 diabetic health outcomes in powerful ways.

These stories highlight several important points. First, they show how dietary changes can have powerful effects on diabetic health outcomes–an improvement over relying solely on diabetic drugs. And second, even though there are many well-designed studies that show that a ketogenic diet is the most effective method for lowering blood sugar, many physicians still don't know about it, and the American Diabetes Association still does not endorse it. We find this puzzling and frustrating, to say the least, and it's part of the reason for creating this book.

Keith R. Runyan, MS, MD

In 1998, at the age of thirty-eight, I was diagnosed with type 1 diabetes, also called latent autoimmune diabetes in adults (LADA). Once the diagnosis was made, I treated my diabetes with multiple insulin injections and frequent blood-sugar monitoring with the advice of endocrinologists along the way. Neither I nor my endocrinologists gave any thought to a change in diet since I was already following a "healthy" dietary regimen as recommended by the American Diabetes Association (ADA). We were pleased that my hemoglobin A1c (HbA1c) tests were hovering between 6.5% and 7% most of the time. Although my HbA1c values were in the ADA-recommended range for diabetics (6.5%–7%), they were certainly not in the normal range for nondiabetics (which is something closer to 4.2%–5.6%). With those values, there was no assurance that I would not develop long-term diabetic complications at some point.

I was having two to five hypoglycemic episodes each week, which I thought were just part of having fairly well-controlled diabetes. My hypoglycemic symptoms ranged from clothes-soaking sweats, rapid and pounding heartbeats, blurred or double vision, transient numbness of skin, and many other symptoms that varied from episode to episode. The most bothersome were the mental symptoms of hypoglycemia. These included an inability to recognize that I was hypoglycemic—therefore, I was not aware that I needed to treat it. This also manifested itself as being argumentative with my family when they told me to take sugar when I felt I did not need any.

Hypoglycemia was an embarrassing event since it meant a lack of control, and it was worsened by the fact that I am a physician and should have all the resources and knowledge to avoid it. More importantly, hypoglycemia can be life-threatening, and although I never lost consciousness, had a seizure, needed assistance, or had to be hospitalized, there was no assurance that any of those things would not happen while I was treating my diabetes using conventional therapy.

I was constantly thinking about how I was feeling and if how I felt could be yet another symptom of hypoglycemia. While lying down to sleep, I wondered whether I would wake up in the night in a sweat from yet another episode of low blood sugar—or not wake up at all! There was a three- to four-month period when my glucose meter was unknowingly reading falsely high. This caused me to overdose insulin, which resulted in nightmarish hypoglycemic episodes so severe that I felt I might die. Fortunately, I was able to manage them myself without needing assistance. I finally purchased a new glucose meter, which put an end to the death-defying episodes. After those experiences, I checked the meter reading against laboratory glucose results, purchased new meters on a more regular basis, and sought out the most accurate meters to purchase.

What I didn't know then was that controlling diabetes with the ADA's high-carbohydrate diet without having recurrent hypoglycemia is impossible. After all, who would have imagined that respected diabetes experts would recommend an impossible task? Do you think I'm still angry? You bet. Having recurrent symptomatic hypoglycemia is certainly not a good way to go through life, especially since it can be avoided!

In August 2007, at the age of forty-seven, I decided to start exercising; I knew I had a chronic disease that might be helped by regular exercise. I decided to start training regularly to complete a sprint triathlon: a 0.9-mile swim, a 10-mile bike, and a 3.1-mile run. Having a goal provided additional motivation for me. I completed my first sprint-distance triathlon in December 2007. After a few years of increasing the distance of the triathlon events, I contemplated doing the full ironman distance triathlon. I started looking into how to keep my body fueled and my blood sugars near normal for the duration of the event, particularly since sugar is the primary fuel used by most athletes during a long-distance triathlon. I was consuming sugar in order to prevent hypoglycemia to the point that I was having hyperglycemia (high blood sugars) more often than not. My HbA1c, a test of average blood sugar over time, had increased to as high as 7.9% as a result, and I feared that it would reverse any benefit of exercise.

In 2011, I signed up to enter an ironman distance triathlon that consisted of a 2.4-mile swim, a 112-mile bike ride, and a 26.2-mile marathon run. Due to my frequent hyperglycemia while consuming sugar, and the constant threat of hypoglycemia, I felt I needed a new approach. That same year, I was listening to a triathlon podcast, IM Talk, hosted by John Newsom and Bevan James Eyles, in which they interviewed Loren Cordain, PhD. That interview introduced me to the concept of diseases of Western civilization. Briefly stated, people who have never been exposed to foods created by agriculture and technology (mainly highly refined sugars and starches, including sweets, flour, white rice, and fruit preserves) rarely develop chronic diseases like dental caries, diabetes, hypertension, heart disease, obesity, dementia, cancer, appendicitis, and peptic ulcers. As a physician, this came as quite a shock to me. One would think that physicians who spend their entire careers treating these chronic diseases would have been taught this in medical school. Soon after, I heard Jimmy Moore's Livin' la Vida Low Carb podcast interview with Dr. Richard K. Bernstein, a diabetes specialist in New York who also had type 1 diabetes. After obtaining one of the first blood-glucose meters available, he discovered by trial and error that carbohydrates had the greatest influence on his blood sugars and that a ketogenic diet containing less than 30 grams carbohydrate per day normalized his blood-sugar levels with a much reduced insulin dosage.

From the tenets of *The Paleo Diet*, as described by Dr. Cordain, I placed more emphasis on using real whole foods and paid more attention to the source of foods. I added grass-fed beef; free-range, pastured chicken; pork; liver; and wild fish to my diet. One can have success with conventionally sourced foods, but I appreciated some of the significant differences that grass-fed and pastured foods had to offer.

Still skeptical that conventional medicine could possibly be so wrong, I was on a mission to both verify what Dr. Cordain was saying and to learn more about how nutrition affects health and disease. I read Gary Taubes's book *Good Calories, Bad Calories* on the history of diseases of Western civilization, the origin of the low-fat diet, lipid-heart and carbohydrate hypotheses, and the evidence supporting the role of dietary refined carbohydrates and sugar in the causation of chronic diseases. I read Dr. Bernstein's *Diabetes Solution*, which described his method of using the ketogenic diet to treat diabetes, and many other books and articles, including many cited in this book. I wanted to make sure that the information I was obtaining was accurate since I was changing my own treatment in opposition to current medical convention.

I also utilized information from *The Art and Science of Low Carbohydrate Living* and *The Art and Science of Low Carbohydrate Performance* by Stephen Phinney, MD, PhD, and Jeff Volek, PhD, RD. When I learned that their information was accurate, I became angry. Why had I not taken the initiative to find this out for myself sooner? Why didn't the world's leading diabetes experts and organizations find this out or mention it as an option? Why didn't the research-funding organizations support studies to test the carbohydrate hypothesis? How could so many scientists and physicians come to believe that a diet with six to eleven daily servings of bread, cereal, rice, and pasta was a "healthy" diet, especially for people with diabetes? After all, those people are the most intolerant of high-carbohydrate foods. In addition, the practice of consuming large amounts of refined foods never existed on the planet until a few hundred years ago. How could humans adapt to them in such a short time on the evolutionary time scale?

So, on February 8, 2012, I started my new lifestyle: a ketogenic diet added to the resistance training, swimming, biking, and running that I had started in 2007. From what I learned reading *The Paleo Diet*, I had already eliminated milk, grains, sugar, starchy legumes, and all processed foods in November 2011.

Following *The Paleo Diet* plan led to a 45% reduction in my mealtime insulin dose but no improvement in my average blood sugar, nor any reduction in hypoglycemic episodes. I needed carbohydrate restriction added to the mix. In order to reduce my carbohydrate intake to 25 to 35 grams per day, I eliminated potatoes and fruit except for a few occasional strawberries or blueberries. To replace calories from the carbohydrates that I eliminated, I increased my dietary fat using small amounts of coconut and olive oils and butter. I simultaneously reduced my insulin doses (both long-acting and short-acting insulins) from about fifty-four units a day to about thirty-five units a day over the next month or so, but I continued to adjust the insulin dose based on my blood-sugar readings and exercise. The variables I tracked included insulin doses, exercise type and duration, and fat intake based on appetite and energy expenditure. The constants I sought to maintain included the ketogenic diet with moderate protein and low-carbohydrate intake, keeping my blood sugar as close to normal as I could safely accomplish, i.e., avoiding hypoglycemia.

Once I adapted to the ketogenic diet, I was able to increase my training distances without needing to eat significant amounts of sugar. I developed the habit of carrying both insulin and glucose tablets with me, just in case, but I rarely needed either of them. I no longer feared hypoglycemia, even while exercising, and my hyperglycemia improved markedly.

On October 20th, 2012, I completed the Great Floridian Triathlon, an ironman distance event, in fifteen and a half hours with no need for any glucose, sugar, or food, using only my body-fat reserves for energy. I had no hypoglycemia, but I did have mild hyperglycemia that I did not treat with insulin because I was expecting my blood sugar to fall at some point during the event. My blood sugar at the end of the event was 156 mg/dL.

My HbA1c improved gradually, from 6.5% on average before the ketogenic diet to 5.6% in the first year on the ketogenic diet. In 2013, it remained at 5.6% and, in 2014, came down to 5.1% with an average blood glucose of 85 mg/dL. This resulted in more hypoglycemia, albeit without symptoms (more on that later); subsequently, I have accepted a near-normal blood glucose—around 95 mg/dL—in exchange for fewer hypoglycemic episodes.

My blood tests have improved in the manner typically seen on a ketogenic diet. Triglycerides decreased from an average of 76 to 65 mg/dL; HDL cholesterol increased from an average of 61 to 90 mg/dL; the triglyceride/HDL ratio decreased from 1.31 to 0.72; and the calculated LDL cholesterol increased from an average of 103 to 162 mg/dL but later came down to 132 mg/dL. The hs-CRP (high-sensitivity

C-reactive protein, a marker of inflammation) decreased from 3.2 to 0.7 mg/L. I have chronicled my personal results on my blog: http://ketogenicdiabeticathlete.wordpress.com.

Today, I have no complications from diabetes, and with my improved glycemic control, my outlook on life has improved dramatically.

Carsten Thomsen

Hello. My name is Carsten, and December 13, 1975, is when my long journey dealing with type 1 diabetes began. On December 12, I had eaten an entire large pizza, a box of fried chicken, and a half-gallon of ice cream. After consuming all that food I lost five pounds while sleeping.

My parents immediately took me to the doctor to have me checked out. When my blood sugar was tested, and the result was 425, it was pretty easy for the doctor to make his diagnosis: I had type 1 juvenile diabetes mellitus.

I was sent to see a dietician to fill me in on how I should be eating as a type 1 diabetic. I was told to eat the proper amount of food by weighing all of my portions, to eat very little fat or protein, and to eat lots of fruits and carbohydrates.

For the next ten years, I tried my best to follow the standard recommendations for keeping my blood sugar under control. I ate what they told me to eat (standard American Diabetes Association recommendations), exercised when I could, and kept taking my insulin shots. The problem was that I kept gaining weight; I was always tired, and I was taking huge amounts of insulin.

Looking back on that diet now, I'm surprised that I'm not dead.

I followed that plan for a long time. I constantly fought weight gain and could barely keep my blood-sugar levels under control. At the time, I was taking one hundred units of insulin a day. For those of you who don't take insulin, one hundred units is a major amount. Over a period of time, I also gained thirty-five pounds.

I've worked in the health profession as an environmental health specialist for the last thirty years. My career has enabled me to keep close track of information related to medical conditions, nutrition, and the effects of the environment on health. About twenty-five years ago, I discovered that the traditional way I was taught to control my diabetes was certainly not the only way. I've spent thousands of hours doing research on what I could do to live a healthier life. I took the best available knowledge and applied it to myself.

During my research, I found a few diabetes specialists who were promoting a totally different approach by controlling diabetes with diet. These specialists evaluated medical information on how diabetics were treated before insulin was available. Before insulin treatment, diabetes was treated by eating meals consisting mostly of fats, with some proteins and low-carbohydrate vegetables, which controlled the blood-sugar levels.

After reading the research, the experiences I was having with a high carbohydrate diet made a lot of sense to me. I decided to eat large amounts of fat, small amounts of protein, and some low-carbohydrate vegetables. After following that diet for several months, I was amazed at the results.

By removing almost all of the carbohydrates from my diet, my blood-sugar levels became very stable. I was not hungry all the time, and, best of all, the amount of insulin I needed dropped by almost 80%. I was excited with my results, and I wanted to share them with my doctor. I told him about the diet I was using, and he had a fit. He informed me that if I continued eating all that fat and protein I would become obese and probably die of a heart attack or kidney disease.

I was feeling so good though, I persisted with my newfound diet. To be cautious and make sure I wasn't hurting myself, I had my cholesterol, triglycerides, and kidney-function levels checked frequently. To my doctor's subdued amazement, my overall cholesterol level dropped, my good (HDL) cholesterol level increased, my triglyceride level dropped like a rock, and my kidney-function levels did not change at all. I've now been on this diet for about twenty years, and all of my blood markers and kidney-function levels have continued in the "very healthy" ranges.

I hope I have conveyed to you through this brief story about my life with diabetes how much better I feel and how much healthier I am after cutting out all those carbohydrates from my diet. I'm sure not everybody will have the same results I've had through my journey, but I've been totally blessed with minimal impact on my health—even after forty years of being a type 1 diabetic. I urge anyone who has type 1 or type 2 diabetes to give a low-carbohydrate, high-fat diet a chance. By doing so, your overall health can be changed in wonderful, amazing ways.

Andrew Koutnik

I was diagnosed with type 1 diabetes when I was sixteen years old. I have since experienced hundreds of hypo- and hyperglycemic moments.

A few years into managing my disease, at age twenty, I accidently miscalculated my insulin bolus. I injected two and a half times more fast-acting insulin than I needed and my blood glucose rapidly dropped into the 20s. My jaw started to lock up. I lost the ability to think critically and comprehend language. At that time, I was by myself and I remember vividly the moment I looked at the TV and realized I could not comprehend what was being said on The Discovery Channel. In this moment, I had the unfortunate glimpse into the mental terror that transpires when the world around you is incomprehensible and you are aware of it. Out of fear, I consumed more than 350 grams of carbohydrates within fifteen minutes via various foods (protein bars, apples, bananas, ice cream, Gatorade, and sugar tablets) and my blood glucose hovered between 40–50 mg/dL for two hours before stabilizing. I then tried, unsuccessfully, to expel the excess food from my stomach in an attempt to ease the distension and acidity I was feeling. The post-hypoglycemic exhaustion was unbearable, so I set an alarm for two hours and fell asleep knowing I would have a hyperglycemic rebound. I woke up at 500 mg/dL. Ironically, I then began the reverse twelve-hour journey of slowly lowering the severe hyperglycemia that followed. Luckily this was my most severe hypoglycemic event. It didn't result in a hospitalized coma, although I unfortunately know many type 1 diabetics for whom it has. Fatalities are rare, but can occur.

Nutritional approaches that significantly reduce glycemic fluctuations are a giant step towards reducing these events that are a reality for type 1 diabetics. Fortunately, for me, hypo- and hyperglycemic moments have been reduced dramatically with better control over my diet and lifestyle. Ultimately, everyone must find an approach that helps them achieve the best blood glucose management and quality of life. For me, my best blood glucose management has always been with low-carbohydrate diets.

The dynamic nature of insulin sensitivity is hard to appreciate if you are not a type 1 diabetic. Carbohydrate intake and insulin boluses can make blood glucose management a daily guessing game. Ultimately, the higher the carbohydrates, the higher the risk in blood glucose fluctuations when predicting insulin dosages.

Decreasing my carbohydrate intake drastically improved my blood glucose management and lowered my overall insulin requirements 50% to 66%. As a result, I have become much more effective as a professional, friend, family member, and relationship partner; all of which can be adversely affected through poor glycemic control.

Since being diagnosed with type 1 diabetes, I have been lucky enough to have had guidance from people in diverse backgrounds: endocrinologist/ADA president, professional athlete with type 1 diabetes, scientist/strength coach, etc. These different perspectives helped give me insight into an array of dietary and insulin approaches. Through my work as a researcher in biomedical science, I have studied the ketogenic diet and I am familiar with the data that show it can be a safe and effective tool for managing health and certain chronic diseases if applied correctly.

Although finding a plan that works is a highly individualized process, low carbohydrate approaches, like the one laid out in this book, have helped me and many other type 1 diabetics personalize a lifestyle approach to effectively manage their disease.

Carl Martin

Men's Health did a story on me once, then they never published it. Guess they were worried about sponsors. The story was about how I controlled my diabetes with diet and exercise and no meds.

I am sure I had diabetes for at least a decade before diagnosing myself approximately fifteen years ago. I was getting physicals from my doctor every year, but my blood glucose was never checked. I got very sick; I was seriously ill. I had all the classic symptoms, so I went to my doctor and told him I had diabetes. There was no good advice from him, only prescriptions for drugs to take. I have had many doctors over the years and have received no good advice from any of them. No doctor ever told me the most important thing I needed to do—lose weight and cut the carbs out of my diet.

A friend of mine who was also diabetic gave me the best advice I ever got from anyone about how to control my diabetes. He told me to lose fifty pounds, and the symptoms would go away. I went on the late great Dr. Robert Atkins diet. I lost eighty-five pounds, and the symptoms did go away. I was always a bicycle commuter and got plenty of exercise. I would say extreme exercise. Exercise alone is not enough. It has to be diet and exercise to be effective. I have always ridden a bicycle twenty miles a day commuting to work.

One of the first things I learned was that I had to take control of my own health. Doctors never provided me with anything positive about controlling my health. My very best source of information came from David Mendosa's diabetic website. David is fabulous. I also have been friends over the web with Jimmy Moore since he started his blog.

Over the years, the weight would come back, and I would look for ways to be able to eat a more normal diet—the magic pill. I tried all the new latest medications: Byetta, Januvia, Victosa, and many others; I finally started Lantus insulin. They all were effective for a while but not for long. The blood sugar would start creeping up. The drugs would initially work but not for long. The drugs all stopped working. Insulin stopped working. I did not like taking insulin. I know how damaging it was to my body.

My weight was going up, but, more importantly, my blood sugar was going way up. So I went back on my ketogenic diet. My blood sugar instantly dropped to normal, even below normal, I never expected such dramatic results, even though I had years of experience with low-carb diets. I have been off insulin for a while now and have never had better blood-glucose levels. My weight is slowly going down, and I have pulled a notch in my belt. Naturally I feel better. I should have been most worried about my health, but I was also determined that I was not going to buy larger-size clothes!

I ran across Ellen's site and think it is excellent. I am amazed how much great information is now available on the Internet. When I first discovered I had diabetes, about the only good information I could find on the web was from David Mendosa and Jimmy Moore. David and I took the same journey with diabetic control. We started Byetta at the same time, when it was new. David dropped the drugs and went to very low-carb eating and cured his diabetes.

Sandy Bahr

I was diagnosed with type 2 diabetes in December 2009, with blood sugars from the 180s to the 220s (10–12.3 mmol) and an A1c of 8.6. It was certainly not unexpected, given my family history and my gestational diabetes during my pregnancies.

When I went to my first diabetes education class, I was the only newly diagnosed diabetic there who was not on medication yet (thanks to a doctor who believed in me). That was my last diabetes education class. The idea of eating corn flakes and sugar-laden low-fat yogurt just struck me as wrong. It has been a journey—and a lot of trial and error!

I went pretty much grain free and low carb in 2011, but I still couldn't get my morning blood sugar down, and my after-meal blood sugar was 130 to 140 mg/dL. This was not acceptable to me as I remembered reading in Dr. Bernstein's book *Diabetes Solution* that blood sugars over 130 would continue to cause organ damage.

In December of 2012, I read the book *The Art and Science of Low Carbohydrate Living* by Stephen Phinney and Jeff Volek. It has become my diabetes bible. I began the ketogenic-diet program described in their book, and a miracle took place in my life. Within five days, my blood sugars normalized, and I was seeing a fasting blood sugar under 100 and after-meal blood sugars in the 90s. I was pinching myself in disbelief!

I had my yearly "preventative" exam in January 2015, after twenty-six months on the ketogenic diet. I say that because I no longer have to have diabetes follow-up exams. My doctor has declared me to be no longer diabetic "on paper" (as she says). She was completely blown away by my labs and could hardly believe my numbers:

- Fasting blood glucose on day of testing was 74 (4.1 mmol), and HbA1c was 5.3.
- Homocysteine was down to 9.8 from 11.8 in 2013. This is a marker for heart disease. Below 10 is fine. Over 13 or so is concerning.

All of my liver enzymes were improved over the previous three years. So much for the propaganda saying that a high-fat diet causes fatty liver!

My total cholesterol of 222 was borderline but it was higher due to the higher "healthy" HDL. My LDL of 106 was near optimal (down from 144), and my HDL of 92 was optimal (up 40 points from last year). More importantly, my triglyceride level of 120 was normal (145 last year). My ratios improved as well:

- Total cholesterol/HDL ratio (preferably <5.0, ideally <3.5) was 2.41—ideal.
- LDL/HDL ratio (preferably <5.0, ideally <2.0) was 1.152—ideal.
- Triglycerides/HDL ratio (preferably <4, ideally <2) was 1.304—ideal.

I "teach" the ketogenic diet for use in diabetes in two Facebook groups, and many more are now finding the same success that I have found. You can find my personal blog at http://ketodiabetes.blogspot.com.

Clair Schwan

Having been diagnosed several years ago with type 2 diabetes, my doctor recommended Metformin as a course of treatment, along with vigorous exercise and a diet emphasizing complex carbohydrates. I generally went along with the diet and exercise recommendations but insisted that I wasn't going to use any medication to address my higher-than-normal fasting blood-glucose readings. After all, I wasn't a flaming diabetic with blood sugar readings in the 200 to 300 range, but rather in the low 100s. I figured that I ought to be able to fix this on my own. I also considered that if I were to use medication as a crutch, I might needlessly create a dependency on medication for a condition that I essentially gave to myself through my own neglect. I thought it was entirely possible to rid myself of this condition by simply being a better caretaker of me.

As a first step, I generally followed a low-carbohydrate diet, but I wasn't doing anything precise or scientific. Nevertheless, the results were encouraging. My fasting blood sugars were in the high normal to pre-diabetic range, typically 91 to 118. Based on these preliminary trials, my physician confirmed that my condition was indeed reversible, if only I paid closer attention to diet and exercise.

After learning more about a special type of low-carbohydrate diet, known as a ketogenic diet, I began to understand more about the science behind it, and I started to appreciate that implementation had to be done with some level of precision in order to be effective. My blood sugars were stubbornly in the pre-diabetic range, while all the rest of my blood work was normal. So, the time had come to apply a more scientific approach to my diet.

I undertook a twenty-three-day application of the ketogenic diet as a trial, with strict application of criteria for fat, protein, and carbohydrate intake. As a result, my fasting blood sugar dropped a total of 53 points, from a high of 125 to a low of 72. A normal fasting blood-sugar reading of 88 was achieved on day six of the diet, and during the last two weeks of the trial, my average morning blood-sugar reading was 86. In addition to a reduction in fasting blood sugars, I lost a much needed twenty-two pounds and had to cut back my blood-pressure medications to one quarter the dosage because my blood pressure was significantly lower as well. All of this occurred simply because of a change in diet; I didn't do anything special in terms of exercise.

During my trial application, I learned many things about the ketogenic diet that are important. First, although the percentage of fat intake is relatively high when compared with protein and carbohydrate, since fat has more than twice the calories per gram, it's relatively easy to meet fat requirements by simply going a bit heavy on butter and bacon grease when preparing meals. Second, it's clear that fat doesn't make you fat; instead, it's a great alternate fuel to replace the glucose that most of us are conditioned to use. Third, keeping protein at a modest level prevents conversion of excess protein to glucose during gluconeogenesis, which occurs while you sleep. Fourth, even raw carrots cause a considerable increase in fasting blood-sugar readings, so I now avoid them. Fifth, after a couple of weeks on the diet, hunger seems to disappear and that makes staying on the diet much easier.

Based on what I've seen, heard, read, and experienced, it's clear to me that no single formula for lowering and stabilizing blood sugars will work for everyone. Nevertheless, the ketogenic diet has many clear benefits to offer to those of us who are carbohydrate intolerant. It will be an important tool in my health care toolbox from now on.

2

Ketogenic Diets and Diabetes

Now that we've shared some personal success stories, let's explore some specific information on how ketogenic diets work, how diabetes works, and how ketogenic diets can improve diabetic health outcomes.

What Is a Ketogenic Diet?

All diets consist of three key macronutrients: fats, such as butter and oil; carbohydrates, found in sweets and starchy foods; and protein, found in meats, dairy, and nuts. A ketogenic diet is high in fat, moderate in protein, and very low in carbohydrate.

A ketogenic diet restricts carbohydrate intake to about 2% to 10% of total calories. In contrast, the United States Department of Agriculture (USDA) guidelines for a standard American diet (SAD) recommend that 45% to 65% of calories come from carbohydrates, the nutrient to which a person with diabetes is most intolerant.

The difference between these two diets is in their cellular-fuel effects. The high quantities of carbohydrate-containing foods consumed on the SAD are broken down into large amounts of blood sugar. This, in turn, causes a rise in the need for insulin, a hormone that acts to push sugar from the bloodstream into our cells where it can be stored or broken down into energy for the body. The more carbohydrates eaten, the more insulin is needed to deal with the resulting elevations in blood glucose.

In contrast, when carbohydrate intake is restricted and protein intake is moderate, blood glucose and insulin needs are reduced, and this causes a biochemical adaptation and shift toward the use of fat instead of glucose to fuel body cells. As a result, stored fat is more easily liberated from fat tissue, and there is an increase in ketogenesis, a process in which the liver creates ketone bodies from fatty acids and releases them into the bloodstream so that the brain, muscles, and other tissues can use them as an alternate fuel. Ketone bodies are metabolic byproducts that result when the body shifts fuel sources and burns fat more readily than carbohydrates. We are accustomed to hearing that carbohydrates are the body's preferred fuel, but the truth is, the human body is capable of thriving on fats and ketones.

The two- to three-week process of restricting carbohydrates to increase fat- and ketone-producing enzymes is called fat-adaptation and keto-adaptation. Once the body is "keto-adapted" and has made the switch from using glucose to using fat and ketones as the primary fuel, that person is said to be in "nutritional ketosis." Ketosis is an evolutionary adaptation to food scarcity[3]. In fact, the biochemical effect of a ketogenic diet is very similar to the effect of a complete fast from food. When food is unavailable, the most crucial task of the body's energy systems is to provide glucose to fuel the brain. No glucose for the brain equates to no life. In addition, muscle mass has to be protected so that a hunt for food can continue. Ketosis is the perfect solution. Once keto-adapted, the body uses fatty acids and ketones from stored fat to fuel most cells, and glucose needs are reduced. Otherwise, if the body were to continue to depend on glucose alone, most of the muscle tissue would be quickly consumed. This is because during prolonged food deprivation, muscle is broken down into its amino-acid building blocks, which are then converted to glucose for the brain.

In addition, there are some profound and positive health effects[4] when the body uses ketones as its primary fuel source. For instance, cellular inflammation and free-radical activity are reduced. There is also less glycation damage. Glycation and free-radical activity contribute to the development and progression of a long list of diabetic complications, including kidney damage[5], blindness[6], peripheral nerve damage[7], and heart disease[8]. It's not such a leap in logic to consider that our bodies are meant to run on ketones, given the positive health effects they bestow.

The antioxidant and anti-inflammatory effects of nutritional ketosis are why calorie restriction, fasting, and ketogenic diets have such beneficial effects on human health. In fact, nutritional ketosis and ketone bodies themselves are being studied extensively as a treatment for many metabolic diseases. A growing number of research papers[9] have been published on the anti-inflammatory effect of ketones on conditions such as epilepsy, multiple sclerosis, ALS, Parkinson's disease, Alzheimer's disease, head trauma, cancer, cardiovascular disease, autism, migraine headaches, stroke, depression, acne, and, of course, diabetes.[10]

The takeaway here is that the ketogenic diet is not a fad. It is a potent regulator of metabolic derangement, and, when formulated and implemented correctly, it can be extremely effective, especially in the treatment of diabetes.

What Is Diabetes?

Diabetes is a group of diseases that are characterized by high levels of glucose or sugar in the bloodstream resulting from either a lack of insulin or dysfunctional insulin signaling. According to the American Diabetes Association's 2014 National Report,[11] over twenty-one million Americans were diagnosed with diabetes, and another eight million have diabetes but remain undiagnosed; these numbers are predicted to increase dramatically in the future. People with uncontrolled diabetes develop serious complications leading to heart disease, stroke, kidney failure, amputations, blindness, and death.

There are several different types of diabetes.[12] Type 1 diabetes mellitus (T1DM) and type 2 diabetes mellitus (T2DM) are the most common. T1DM is an autoimmune disease that primarily affects children, adolescents, and young adults. If it occurs in adults, it is designated as latent autoimmune diabetes in adults (LADA). In contrast, T2DM primarily affects adults, but the rates of this disease are escalating in younger adults, adolescents, and children. Eighty-five percent of people with T2DM are overweight or obese. The cause of T2DM is severe insulin resistance (resistance to the effect of insulin), which can first manifest as metabolic syndrome and prediabetes. The list below shows pertinent differences between types of diabetes.

Type 1 Diabetes

- Affects children and adolescents
- Autoimmune disease
- Pancreatic beta cells non-functional; no insulin secreted
- Insulin must be injected
- 5%–10% of all diabetes diagnoses

LADA (Latent Autoimmune Diabetes in Adults)

- Affects young adults to elderly
- Autoimmune disease
- Slower destruction of pancreatic beta cells
- Pancreatic beta cells non-functional; no insulin secreted
- Insulin must be injected

Type 2 Diabetes

- Can strike at any age
- Insulin resistance is the defining disease factor
- Obesity is a symptom
- Pancreatic beta cells functional; insulin secreted, sometimes in large amounts
- Non insulin dependent (but may need insulin to control blood sugar)

Although type 1 diabetes (T1DM) results from the autoimmune destruction of the beta cells and the loss of both insulin and amylin secretion, type 2 diabetes (T2DM) is a multisystem disorder that begins with the development of insulin resistance in multiple tissues, including muscle, liver, and adipose tissue, with secondary hyperinsulinemia (excess insulin secretion into the blood), and only in the late stage of the disease does insulin secretion become impaired.

The beta cells are part of a structure called the islet of Langerhans in the pancreas. Insulin and amylin, the hormones that beta cells secrete, regulate the neighboring alpha cells, which secrete a hormone called glucagon, and the delta cells, which produce a hormone called somatostatin. Somatostatin can inhibit both insulin and glucagon secretion. Together, the beta cells, alpha cells, and delta cells carefully regulate blood glucose and regulate metabolism throughout the body. When the beta cells become dysfunctional or are destroyed, this elegant regulation is lost, resulting in the symptoms of diabetes.

Insulin is a key hormone that controls not only blood glucose but also many other aspects of fuel metabolism. Insulin's main function is to transfer glucose from the blood into body cells so that it can be metabolized for energy or stored as glycogen, a larger molecule found primarily in the liver and skeletal muscle. For people with a fully functioning pancreas, this transfer and storage process happens when food is ingested and metabolized. It may take several hours for all food to be broken down and absorbed. Once all of the incoming food is stored or metabolized for energy, insulin has completed its job and blood-sugar levels begin to drop.

If the next meal is skipped or delayed, the alpha cells of the pancreas secrete glucagon. Glucagon signals the liver to break down stored glycogen into glucose and release it into the blood to maintain normal blood-sugar levels. The liver may also produce glucose from various "precursor" molecules in a process called gluconeogenesis. In addition, fatty acids may be produced for fuel as the rate of ketogenesis increases.

Diabetes is diagnosed when blood-sugar levels rise above normal, either because the pancreas is damaged by an autoimmune attack and stops making insulin, as in type 1 diabetes, or because the body becomes insensitive to insulin's message (insulin resistance), as in type 2 diabetes. The symptoms of diabetes include the following:

- Polyuria (frequent urination)
- Polydipsia (drinking lots of fluids)
- Thirst and dry mouth
- Extreme fatigue
- Blurry vision
- Cuts and bruises that are slow to heal
- Tingling, pain, or numbness in the hands and feet
- Hunger, weight loss

The danger of diabetes is in the lack of insulin or resistance to insulin that results in a blood-sugar "roller coaster" effect. High blood sugar (hyperglycemia) contributes to glycation damage and long-term complications, and low blood sugar (hypoglycemia) can cause a loss of consciousness or death if the brain runs out of fuel. In the next section, we'll explore these conditions in more detail.

Blood Glucose, Hyperglycemia, and Hypoglycemia

As we learned earlier, glucose is a simple sugar that your cells use to make energy. It's created from the breakdown or metabolism of foods that contain carbohydrates (starches and sugars) and, to a lesser extent, protein foods such as meat and eggs. Glucose is utilized in the body through the action of insulin, a hormone that "pushes" glucose into body cells so it can be used to make adenosine triphosphate (ATP), the energy currency of the human body.

Blood glucose is a measure of the amount of glucose (sugar) in your bloodstream at any one time. Normally, the human body has mechanisms in place to maintain the amount of glucose in the bloodstream in a very narrow range. At any one time, normal blood sugar amounts to a little less than 5 grams[13] or one teaspoon of sugar. Mathematically, this works out to a range of about 83–99 mg/dL, the "normal" range of blood sugar.

For people with diabetes, blood-sugar levels are constantly out of the normal range. Most of the time, blood glucose is too high, a condition known as hyperglycemia. A diabetic with uncontrolled blood sugars may have two to ten times the normal amount of blood glucose. Hyperglycemia is responsible for most of the damage that results in long-term diabetic complications. The damage is done through a process called glycation in which blood sugar "sticks" to various body tissues, causing dysfunction. Because diabetic blood sugars are higher than normal for longer periods of time, more glycation damage is done. Glycation is measured using two tests. The first is called the hemoglobin A1C test (HbA1c), which measures glycation in red blood cells. While a finger-stick measurement of blood glucose is a snapshot of one moment in time, the HbA1c test is a longer-term measurement and can be thought of as reflecting average blood glucose over the previous two- to three-month span. The second test is called a fructosamine test, which measures glycation in a blood protein called albumin over the previous two- to three-week period.

Diabetics can also experience low blood sugar or hypoglycemia, and this can be even more dangerous. Without blood sugar, human body systems cease to function; in the case of the human brain, a lack of blood sugar can result in a loss of consciousness, seizures, coma, and death. Hypoglycemia is a constant danger for diabetics, especially those using insulin, a sulfonylurea, or a glinide drug to manage excess blood sugar.

In the next section, we will explore how different food choices affect blood sugar and insulin levels, and why it's important for those with diabetes to minimize carbohydrate intake.

Food Choices, Blood Sugar, and Insulin

For people with diabetes, the dynamics of blood sugar and insulin are a primary focus each day. Controlling the long-term complications of diabetes is dependent upon managing insulin and its effect on blood sugar. This is why the types and amounts of foods eaten are important, and this is where a ketogenic diet makes a difference. Let's take a closer look at how food choices affect blood sugar and insulin needs.

Foods in the human diet are composed of three important macronutrients: fats, carbohydrates, and proteins. Upon digestion in the body, each of these macronutrients has a different effect on blood sugar and insulin needs as described below.

Most dietary fats and oils are in the form of triglycerides (TG), which can be either saturated (butter, coconut oil), monounsaturated (olive oil), or polyunsaturated (vegetable oils such as safflower or soybean). Of the three macronutrients, dietary fat has the least stimulatory effect on blood sugar. Dietary fat also slows the rate of absorption of carbohydrates and therefore mitigates somewhat their effect on blood glucose. The need for insulin is lower.

Proteins are primarily found in foods such as meats, eggs, poultry, fish, and some plant foods (soy, nuts, and beans). During digestion, proteins are broken down into smaller units called amino acids. Dietary protein has a moderate effect on blood sugar and requires a moderate dose of insulin. In a study by Symons et al. at the University of Texas,[14] a 113-gram protein meal increased serum insulin levels by 50%, at most.

Carbohydrates are found in foods such as dairy, fruits, vegetables, beans, grains (wheat, rice, corn), and all starchy or sweet foods. Upon digestion, carbohydrates are broken down into simple sugars (glucose, galactose, and fructose). Dietary carbohydrates have the greatest effect on blood sugar. Carbohydrates eaten in any amount or form will raise blood sugar and necessitate large doses of insulin to counteract rapid blood-sugar elevations. Large doses of insulin then increase the danger of low blood sugar.

The amount of each of these macronutrients in the diet is important as well, as each has a role to play in health maintenance.

Fat is a structural component of all mammalian cell walls and many hormones; it also provides a major fuel source for the body. Dietary fat requirements are largely determined by body mass, total energy expenditure, and current body-fat stores. Active individuals will require more dietary fat intake, while obese individuals will require less dietary fat intake since fat already stored in the body can act as a source of energy.

Protein is primarily used as a structural and functional element in the body and is only secondarily used as a fuel. Dietary protein intake should be based on lean body mass—or goal body weight (GBW)—and the level of physical activity pursued. We will explore determining your protein needs in chapter 5.

Carbohydrates are not essential in the diet, so dietary carbohydrate intake can be based on one's carbohydrate tolerance. However, diabetes is a state of profound carbohydrate intolerance, and people with diabetes will gain the most benefit from strictly limiting dietary carbohydrates, usually to about 30–50 grams per day.

Understanding total macronutrient intake will help you determine which foods are the best choices to increase ketosis and lower your blood sugar and insulin needs. We'll talk about customizing macronutrient intake for your individual needs later on. For now, let's get back to nutritional ketosis and why it and the ketogenic diet are so helpful for people with diabetes.

Nutritional Ketosis and Your Brain

Let's explore why a ketogenic diet is better for people with diabetes. Nutritional ketosis is a metabolic state that occurs when a person either fasts or restricts carbohydrate intake. After two to three consistent weeks on a carb-restricted ketogenic diet, the liver adapts to lower glucose and insulin by producing increased quantities of ketone bodies from either dietary fat or fat released from fat cells.

Here's the important part: The liver does this because the human brain must be fueled constantly to stay alive. Any interruption in fuel availability is an emergency for the brain. And while human brains can run on both glucose and ketones, there's a balancing act involved. This issue of balanced fuel sources for the brain is crucial to understanding the positive effect of a ketogenic diet on diabetic health factors.

The crux of it is whether your brain is "carb-adapted" or "keto-adapted." Once this concept is understood, dietary choices begin to make real sense, and the benefits of a ketogenic diet for diabetes can be realized.

Is Your Brain Carb-Adapted or Keto-Adapted?

Let's explore the difference between having a brain that is carb-adapted versus having a keto-adapted brain. Carb-adapted is up first because that's typical for someone consuming a standard American diet.

When a person consumes a high-carbohydrate diet, ketone production in the liver is essentially shut off due to the presence of large amounts of circulating glucose and insulin. Since ketones are unavailable, the brain is dependent on glucose as its only fuel source. We call this a carb-adapted brain since it relies greatly on glucose to function and thrive.

When a carb-adapted brain senses that blood glucose is becoming scarce (such as when food is unavailable or when too much insulin is injected), it has to take countermeasures and an adrenalin rush ensues. The adrenalin rush results in the symptoms of hypoglycemia or low blood sugar. The signal is frantic because, at this point, glucose must be made available from glucose tablets or food that is high in sugar. Otherwise, as glucose levels drop further, the carb-adapted brain can lose consciousness, and, without an intervention of glucagon by injection, glucose levels can drop to a point that results in coma or death.

For example, let's say Ben, a person with type 1 diabetes, prepares a meal with a large amount of carbohydrate. Just before the meal, Ben gives himself a large injection of insulin to counteract the blood-sugar rise that he knows he will experience from the carbohydrate he eats. A few minutes into his meal, he gets a frantic phone call from a friend who needs some immediate help. Ben leaves the house in a hurry and doesn't finish his meal.

Thirty minutes later, the insulin he injected kicks in, and because he didn't eat the amount of carbohydrate he thought he would, the excess insulin drops his blood sugar to dangerously low levels. As he breaks into a sweat and starts to feel weak and dizzy, his friend realizes what is happening and gets him some orange juice to drink. This brings his blood sugar back up and offsets the effects of the excess insulin.

In this case, Ben's liver was unable to break down stored carbohydrate due to the excessive insulin dose. As his blood-glucose levels dropped, his carbohydrate-adapted brain started to lose consciousness. Without the intervention of sugar (juice, glucose tablets, or candy) from outside, his blood sugar could have dropped to a level that resulted in a coma or death. As you can see, a frantic low-blood-sugar warning system is necessary for a carb-adapted brain.

Now consider Lisa, a type 1 diabetic who is on a ketogenic diet. Lisa restricts her carb intake to the same small amount every day. Over time, her liver has increased its ketone production. She has entered a state of "nutritional ketosis." Her blood-ketone levels stay in a range of 0.5–3 mmol/L (mM), and, at this level, the ketones can cross the blood-brain barrier and diffuse into her neurons where they can be metabolized as a fuel source. Since her brain is ketone-adapted, low blood sugar becomes less of an emergency since her brain cells now have an alternate fuel source.

Lisa is able to keep her insulin doses very small because there is no carbohydrate-induced spike in her blood sugars, and this lowers her risk of hypoglycemia. Hence, she very rarely experiences any symptoms of low blood sugar. Lisa has taken her blood sugar at times and noticed it was lower than normal, but she did not feel weak or faint. However, she made sure to correct her glucose reading to >70 mg/dL with a glucose tablet. Being keto-adapted gives her body options for keeping her brain supplied with an energy source.

In the overall evolutionary design of the human body, the ability of the liver to produce ketones is an elegant solution for providing an alternate body fuel when food is unavailable. Fasting and starvation cause the same elevation in ketone production, and, in fact, most people wake up each morning in mild ketosis because they haven't eaten for the past eight to twelve hours. Having a keto-adapted brain is advantageous, and following a ketogenic diet bestows other benefits as well. Let's discuss some of these.

Benefits of a Ketogenic Diet

The benefits of a ketogenic diet are numerous and affect many different body systems. Below are some of the most common reported.

> *Lower insulin doses for diabetics.* The ketogenic diet requires the least amount of insulin compared to any other diabetic dietary therapy. This explains why it's so effective in prevention and treatment of prediabetes and type 1 and type 2 diabetes. For type 1 diabetics, dietary carbohydrate restriction means the input of glucose into the bloodstream is minimized, and this lowers the amount of insulin that needs to be injected. In a 2012 Swedish study, forty-eight people with type 1 diabetes were instructed to follow a 75-gram-per-day low-carbohydrate diet. The results showed that the participants achieved a mean reduction in HbA1c from 7.6% at the start to 6.3% at just three months. After four years, the HbA1c was still only 6.9%. Mean daily mealtime insulin for thirty-six patients was reduced from 23 ± 9 IU at the start to 13 ± 6 IU at one year. Mean daily long-acting insulin was reduced modestly from 19.6 ± 5 IU to 18.6 ± 6 IU in the first year. Hypoglycemic episodes were reduced by 82%, from 2.9 to 0.5 episodes per week.[15]

> *Lower blood pressure.* Ketogenic diets are very effective at reducing blood pressure. If you are taking blood-pressure medications, be aware that this may result in feeling dizzy from too much medication. You may need to reduce your blood-pressure medication, so talk with your doctor about reassessing your medication dosage before you start.

> *Increase in* HDL *cholesterol and reduction in triglycerides.* In most people, following a ketogenic diet will raise HDL cholesterol while lowering triglycerides and total cholesterol.[16] This is actually a

positive change because it improves the ratio of HDL to LDL. Higher HDL levels ($\geq$ 40 mg/dL (men) or $\geq$ 50 mg/dL (women) indicate a lower risk for heart disease. Carbohydrate consumption is a direct driver of triglyceride levels in the blood. As triglycerides rise, heart-disease risks also rise. The less carbohydrate you eat, the lower your triglyceride readings will be. Triglyceride levels < 100 mg/dL are achievable and optimal for persons with diabetes following a ketogenic diet.

> *Lower average blood glucose (both baseline and after meals).* As your carbohydrate intake drops, your fasting and after-meal blood sugars will drop. An average of these measurements can be seen in HbA1c test results. The HbA1c test is a long-term measure (previous two to three months) of average blood sugar. Since a ketogenic diet lowers blood sugar, HbA1c levels should drop over time.

> *Lower levels of inflammation.* The ketogenic diet is anti-inflammatory in that it reduces numerous markers of inflammation including interleukin, tumor necrosis factor-alpha, vascular endothelial growth factor, interferon-c, epidermal growth factor, monocyte chemotactic protein-1, intracellular cellular adhesion molecule-1, vascular cellular adhesion molecule-I, and nuclear factor-kappa B, as shown in a study by Forsythe et al. at the University of Connecticut.[17] A test called the high-sensitivity C-reactive protein (hs-CRP) test is used to measure total body-system inflammation. This test is also a marker for heart-disease risk, since heart disease is linked to high levels of body inflammation. An optimal hs-CRP level is < 1 mg/L. Once you start a ketogenic diet, and your blood sugar and insulin requirements drop, you should see your hs-CRP level drop as well as other markers of inflammation.

> *Reduction of inappropriate hunger and sugar cravings.* Appetite is reduced on a ketogenic diet. It is not exactly known why this occurs. It may be because fuel flow has normalized and cells are receiving adequate energy. You'll notice that at times you may forget

to eat. You may find this is the most amazing part, especially if you struggle with food addiction.

> *Heartburn relief.* Some people who suffer from gastroesophageal reflux disease (GERD) or other heartburn issues notice improvement in their symptoms after starting a ketogenic diet. The results of a study at the University of North Carolina suggests that a very low-carbohydrate diet in obese individuals with GERD can significantly improve symptoms.[18]

> *Less gum and tooth disease.* Carbohydrate consumption feeds oral bacteria like *streptococcus mutans*, which lowers the pH of your saliva and erodes the tooth enamel, leading to tooth decay.[19] After some time on a ketogenic diet, tooth decay issues may improve.

> *Mood stabilization.* The ketogenic diet has been shown in studies to be effective in treating mood disorders such as bipolar disorder[20] and schizophrenia.[21]

> *Reduction of factors associated with cancer.* A ketogenic diet will cause blood-sugar, insulin, and insulin-like growth factor 1 (IGF-1) levels to drop. Elevated levels of these markers are associated with an increased risk of cancer.[22] Hence, lowering them may reduce your risk of developing cancer.

> *Improvement of non-alcoholic fatty liver disease (NAFLD).* The ketogenic diet can improve this condition more effectively than a calorie-restricted diet. A study at the University of Texas Southwestern Medical Center found that after two weeks on a carb-restricted diet, there was a 42% reduction in hepatic triglycerides in persons with NAFLD.[23]

As you can see from the list above, the change of lifestyle required to adopt a ketogenic diet is balanced nicely by the benefits it bestows. In the next section, we'll dismantle some of the common myths and misconceptions about ketogenic diets.

Dietary Myth Busting

Let's look at three of the most widespread myths about the supposed dangers of a ketogenic diet. In explaining how each came to be, we hope to arm you for the next argument you have with someone who thinks your dietary choices are going to "kill you."

Myth #1: Ketosis Is the Same as Ketoacidosis

One of the most prevalent myths about ketogenic diets is that nutritional ketosis is the same as diabetic ketoacidosis (DKA). In reality, they are two distinctly different conditions.

It's not surprising that medical professionals in particular confuse the two conditions. Medical-school biochemistry textbooks only touch on ketone metabolism briefly. Of the 1,030 pages of the eleventh edition of the *Textbook of Medical Physiology*, one page is devoted to ketone metabolism, a third of a page to ketoacidosis, and four sentences to nutritional ketosis. Incidentally, three of those four sentences are factually incorrect.

Diabetic ketoacidosis has little in common with nutritional ketosis. DKA is a dangerous medical condition caused by a deficiency of insulin often in the setting of illness, typically a serious infection. In contrast, during nutritional ketosis, insulin from either internal or external sources regulates ketone production so that an uncontrolled excess does not occur. If your pancreas is making insulin or if you are healthy and injecting correct amounts of insulin to manage your blood sugar, it's unlikely you would ever experience diabetic ketoacidosis.

Patients with T1DM can develop DKA as a result of an infection, most commonly pneumonia or urinary tract infections, other life stressors, noncompliance with insulin therapy, or as a person's first manifestation of T1DM (previously undiagnosed). The infection or stress causes an increase in hormones that drive up blood sugar. Since the person is ill and may not be eating, they may not realize they need to continue taking proper amounts of insulin. In a patient with T2DM, DKA can be precipitated by an acute illness such as a heart attack or an infection or, if insulin dependent, by noncompliance with insulin therapy.

Patients with DKA are typically quite ill and require hospitalization with an intravenous insulin infusion along with intravenous fluids to correct dehydration. Although metabolic acidosis causes numerous enzymatic reactions to malfunction, the primary cause of death is not DKA itself but rather the underlying precipitating causes. The physiological factors that precipitate DKA include:

- Uninhibited ketone synthesis (associated with insulin deficiency)
- An inability to utilize all of the ketones produced
- Excess production of glucose-creating hormones (glucagon, cortisol, epinephrine, and growth hormone), which leads to excessive glucose production by the liver.

The symptoms of DKA include the following:

- Polyuria (frequent urination)
- Polydipsia (drinking lots of fluids)
- Thirst and dry mouth
- Nausea and vomiting
- Abdominal pain
- Confusion
- Heavy or labored breathing
- Fruity breath odor
- Fatigue
- Symptoms related to the precipitating condition

Thus, diabetic ketoacidosis is a serious and potentially life-threatening complication of either insulin-requiring T1DM or T2DM caused by an acute illness, previously undiagnosed diabetes, or noncompliance with insulin therapy. In 30%–40% of children and 20% of adults with T1DM, diabetic ketoacidosis is the initial manifestation of the condition. In patients known to have diabetes, precipitating factors for DKA include infections, intercurrent illnesses, psychological stress, and poor compliance with therapy. Urinary tract infection, pneumonia, and other infections account for 30%–50% of cases. Although diabetic ketoacidosis is a life-threatening condition for type 1 diabetics, and 2%–5% die despite treatment, if medical attention is sought early, the great majority recover completely.

The list below shows the levels of ketone concentrations in various body states to help differentiate between ketosis and ketoacidosis. The first four levels constitute varying degrees of nutritional ketosis while the fifth level is the more dangerous ketoacidosis. In addition, the very high ketone levels associated with ketoacidosis will be accompanied by high blood sugars as well.

- Level 1: Negligible levels after a meal: 0.1 mM
- Level 2: Negligible levels after an overnight fast: 0.3 mM
- Level 3: Ketogenic diet (nutritional ketosis): 0.5 to 6.0 mM
- Level 4: Beyond twenty days of fasting: <10.0 mM
- Level 5: Diabetic ketoacidosis: >15.0 mM

Nutritional ketosis is a normal consequence of the keto-adapted individual who is restricting dietary carbohydrates to between 20 to 50 grams/day. Blood-ketone levels during nutritional ketosis are so low (0.5–3.0 mM) that acidosis does not occur. In contrast, DKA blood-ketone levels are commonly much higher, usually above 15 mM. Following a ketogenic diet or living in a state of nutritional ketosis does not increase the probability of developing DKA. The only factors these two conditions have in common are their first four letters—*k-e-t-o*.

Myth #2: Cholesterol and Saturated Fat Are Unhealthy

Another myth about the ketogenic diet has to do with fat intake and, in particular, the amount of saturated fat allowed. The general warning you may hear is that eating a diet high in animal fat will clog your arteries with cholesterol and cause heart disease, a story called the lipid-heart hypothesis or the diet-heart hypothesis. There is now plenty of evidence to refute the lipid-heart hypothesis, so let's take a look.

It is a fact that there has never been any scientific study published that links dietary cholesterol and saturated-fat intake to heart disease, even after billions of taxpayer dollars have been spent in an attempt to prove it. In fact, a 2010 meta-analysis by Krauss et al. distinctly destroys any link between heart disease and saturated fat.[24] And a study done by Chris Gardner's team at Stanford University shows that low-carb diets actually improve heart-disease markers over other types of diets.[25] And another specific study done at the University of Connecticut showed that a ketogenic diet favorably affects blood test results for heart disease in normal-weight men.[26]

Cholesterol Is Good for You

The truth is that cholesterol is a very important substance in the body. We are composed of one hundred trillion cells, each with a cell membrane that forms a barrier so that substances can be selectively transported across the membrane. Cell membranes are composed almost entirely of proteins and lipids, with an approximate composition of 55% protein, 25% phospholipid (a waxy fat), and 13% cholesterol. Almost every cell can create its own cholesterol, that's how vital it is to our health. Cholesterol is also the starting compound for synthesis of many important steroid hormones such as estrogen, testosterone, progesterone, cortisol, and aldosterone. More importantly, it's an integral part of our brain and is crucial for proper nerve-cell function. Without cholesterol, the human body doesn't do well. People with a disorder called Smith-Lemli-Opitz syndrome have an inborn error in cholesterol synthesis, which results in abnormalities ranging from mild intellectual disability and behavioral problems to physical deformities that are lethal.[27]

USDA Advice on Saturated Fat and Cholesterol

Although the current 2015-2020 recommendations are less stringent, the USDA still recommends that Americans limit dietary cholesterol and saturated fat intake. We are told to limit nutrient-dense foods such as full-fat dairy products and meat and instead consume polyunsaturated oils, a dubious directive at best. This advice is, in part, why so many of us have ended up obese and sick in America. What the USDA doesn't acknowledge is that there is a decided lack of evidence for limiting dietary cholesterol and saturated fat to benefit heart health. A systematic review and meta-analysis published in the Annals of Internal Medicine in March 2014 reported this conclusion:

> *Current evidence does not clearly support cardiovascular guidelines that encourage high consumption of polyunsaturated fatty acids and low consumption of total saturated fats.*[28]

Interestingly, it has been known since the 1950s that dietary cholesterol has little if any effect on blood cholesterol in humans. The cholesterol you get from your diet is much less than what your liver and other cells will make to maintain your body tissues, because cholesterol is a very important and beneficial substance in the body. Cholesterol acts as a repair substance for cellular damage, so if it is elevated, it may mean that inflammation and tissue damage are present. In other words, cholesterol is just the bandage over an underlying problem of inflammation, which is more likely caused by a high-carbohydrate diet.

There are a great many studies showing that a high-carbohydrate diet and elevated blood sugar and insulin are strongly associated with inflammatory heart disease. For instance, consider the link between HbA1c tests and heart disease. In the EPIC study done at the University of Cambridge in the UK, the researchers looked at the relationship between HbA1c test results and the risk of heart attack. The results were very clear: the higher a person's HbA1c levels (i.e., the higher the average blood sugars and glycation events), the higher the risk of heart attack.[29]

Insulin Resistance, Diabetes and Heart Disease

People with poorly controlled T1DM who are consuming a high-carbohydrate diet commonly have undesirable risk markers for heart disease. These markers include elevated total cholesterol and triglycerides, low HDL cholesterol, and elevated levels of small, dense LDL cholesterol, which is a marker of arterial damage and atherosclerosis. This combination of conditions is called dyslipidemia. Insulin resistance and metabolic syndrome are typically part of type 2 diabetes, but, in persons with type 1 diabetes, taking large doses of insulin to compensate for a high-carbohydrate diet and the resulting obesity can result in "double diabetes," the combination of type 1 and type 2 diabetes in the same individual. The following excerpt is from a review article titled "Saturated fat, carbohydrate, and cardiovascular disease" published in the *American Journal of Clinical Nutrition* in 2010:

> *In recent years, there has been increasing concern regarding dietary effects on dyslipidemia, characterized by elevated triglycerides, low concentrations of HDL cholesterol, and increased concentrations of small, dense LDL particles ... This metabolic profile is considered to be a major contributor to increased CVD risk in patients with the metabolic syndrome, insulin resistance, and type 2 diabetes. Both increased adiposity and higher carbohydrate intakes have been shown to increase the magnitude of each of the components of atherogenic dyslipidemia. Carbohydrate restriction under weight-stable conditions reduced total:HDL cholesterol, apolipoprotein B, and the mass of small, dense LDL particles ... Particularly given the differential effects of dietary saturated fats and carbohydrates on concentrations*

of larger and smaller LDL particles, respectively, dietary
efforts to improve the increasing burden of CVD risk asso-
ciated with atherogenic dyslipidemia should primarily
emphasize the limitation of refined-carbohydrate intakes
and a reduction in excess adiposity.[30]

The typical changes seen when changing from a high-carbohydrate diet to a ketogenic diet include an increase in HDL and a reduction in both small, dense LDL and triglyceride levels. In other words, heart-disease risk markers improve as carbohydrate intake drops. You will see these changes demonstrated in many of the studies presented throughout this book.

Myth #3: Carbs Are an Essential Nutrient for Good Health

You'll hear this from many registered dietitians because they have been taught that people should eat at least 130 grams of carbohydrates each day to provide glucose to fuel the brain and avoid hypoglycemia. It's an old way of thinking, and it's just not true scientifically.

Essential nutrients are nutrients that your body cannot make, so they have to be obtained on a daily basis from your diet. There are essential proteins and essential fatty acids, but there is no such thing as an essential carbohydrate. When dietary carbohydrates are restricted, the body relies on fatty acids and ketones for fuel. When the body is in ketosis, it has a "glucose sparing" effect. Skeletal muscles burn fatty acids preferentially, which spares glucose for the brain to use. Once a person is keto-adapted, the brain switches to using ketone bodies for 50%–80% of the fuel it requires; therefore, less glucose is needed.[3] This small amount of glucose needed to fuel the brain during keto-adaptation can be generated internally. Your liver can make all the glucose needed for brain function from glycogen stored in the liver. And, if need be, the body can also make glucose from protein in your food via a process called gluconeogenesis. Hence, carbohydrates are not essential nutrients. Many people, such as the Inuit of Alaska and the

Maasai of Africa, live without them for long periods of time without any negative effect on health or well-being.

The idea that the brain is completely dependent on glucose is only true if you eat at least 130 grams of carbohydrate per day. A high-carb diet results in your brain becoming "carb-adapted." Blood sugar and insulin will rise on such a diet, and your brain won't have access to ketones to use as an alternate fuel since insulin interferes with ketosis.

We find it puzzling that this 130-gram idea continues to influence dietary advice because the Dietary Reference Intakes for Energy, Carbohydrate, Fiber, Fat, Fatty Acids, Cholesterol, Protein, and Amino Acids (Macronutrients) (2005), a document on which dietitians rely heavily for nutritional guidance, makes the following statement on page 275:

> *The lower limit of dietary carbohydrate compatible with life apparently is zero, provided that adequate amounts of protein and fat are consumed.*[31]

Specific Notes for Type 1 Children

About 75% of Type 1 diabetes cases are diagnosed in people younger than eighteen years. Children and adolescents have different treatment needs than adults, as growth and sexual maturity factors make insulin sensitivity and treatment goals a moving target. Currently, the ADA recommends that all pediatric age groups target an HbA1c of less than 7.5%. The ADA bases its recommendation on the results of the Diabetes Control and Complications Trial (DCCT), which indicated that normal blood glucose was more difficult to achieve in the adolescent population and higher blood-glucose values before meals and bedtime were chosen to help avoid hypoglycemia. However, that trial looked at groups in which carbohydrate intake was much higher than what would be recommended on a ketogenic diet. Therefore, this high-carb intake was likely to result in more frequent spikes and crashes of blood sugar, which makes hypoglycemia more likely.

We include this section regarding children with a disclaimer that the research on these issues is not robust. Much of this information is speculative and based, in part, on the results of surveying families who are struggling with diabetes on a daily basis. We share this information because we believe mainstream medical advice in these areas is inaccurate, confusing to parents, and causing unnecessary harm.

Carbohydrate Recommendations for Children

The ADA recommendation for children with T1DM is to follow a meal plan that either uses carbohydrate counting at each meal or constant carbohydrate intake at each meal. For example, a leading childhood diabetes center, which bases its recommendations on ADA guidelines, communicates, "Careful management of carb intake must be a part of any of the programs. It is impossible to eat varying amounts of carbs (without changing the insulin dosage) and keep the blood sugar from fluctuating up or down."[32]

The ADA website suggests that meals should include large amounts of carbohydrates in the form of fruits, vegetables, and whole grains. To make matters more confusing, the ADA also discusses the importance of restricting fat in the diet and not eating too much protein. Although recent ADA position papers highlight "individual control" of carb intake, they also discuss the benefits of whole grains and other carbohydrates, citing studies in which carbohydrate intake made up 50%–55% of calories.[33] On their carb-counting page, the ADA recommends 45 to 60 grams of carbohydrate at each meal, plus snacks of carbohydrate.[34] This kind of carbohydrate load makes it impossible to keep blood-sugar levels and insulin needs from fluctuating wildly, and, since fat and protein are also to be restricted, it's not surprising that families of children with type 1 diabetes are confused on how to proceed.

In contrast, lowering carbohydrate intake, overall and at each meal, stops the blood-sugar spikes and minimizes the need for excess insulin injections to reduce very high blood sugars. It also negates the ADA rationale that a high-carb intake is required to avoid hypoglycemia during the night. Without spikes and crashes from high-carb intake, hypoglycemic episodes are reduced.

Parents can clearly see that the more carbohydrate a child eats, the more his or her blood-sugar levels fluctuate. They may ask their endocrinologist why meals are built around carbohydrates. Many are told that their child "needs" carbohydrates in order to grow, however, there is no scientific evidence for this assertion. In fact, carbohydrates are not needed for growth, and a study done at the University of Cambridge in the UK indicates that the hyperglycemia associated with ADA dietary recommendations causes kidney damage and stunts growth in children with T1DM.[35] And the results of another study published in the *Journal of Pediatric Endocrinology and Metabolism* indicates that lower blood sugars are associated with stronger bones in type 1 children.[36]

Protein Needs for Children

The macronutrient that is critical for adolescent growth is protein, not carbohydrates. Protein from animal-source foods provides micronutrients such as calcium, zinc, B12, iron, and other vitamins and minerals that are needed for growth. For example, a study by Neumann et al. at the UCLA School of Public Health discusses the linear growth problems seen in Kenyan and Mexican children because their diets lack animal protein but are high in carbohydrates and fiber.[37] Part of the issue for these children is that their diets are also low in calories. This points to another benefit of lowering carbohydrates and increasing protein and fat in a child's diet; these foods provide plenty of energy for growth as well.

Although metabolic studies done on children are limited, protein recommendations have been established. A study done at the University of Vienna in Austria looked at protein requirements for children during weight loss and found that protein intake of 1 gram of protein per kilogram of ideal body weight (IBW) resulted in the maintenance of lean muscle mass.[38]

Adult studies have shown a similar range of 1 to 1.5 grams per kg of IBW. Therefore, a target of 1.2 grams per kilogram of IBW is recommended for children with T1DM to support growth. Here's an example for calculating protein intake in ounces for a child with an ideal body weight of 75 pounds. Divide 75 by 2.2 to get the child's weight in kilograms (about 34 kilograms). Then multiply 34 by 1.2 to get a total daily protein target of about 34 to 41 grams. Since a large egg or one ounce of meat, fish, or poultry each contain about 7 grams of protein, this works out to about 6 ounces of meat, fish, poultry, or egg per day for a 75-pound child.

Finally, many diabetic educators don't talk about bolusing insulin for protein intake. This is most likely because the high-carbohydrate intake recommendation masks the need to bolus for protein. Parents who decide to implement a low-carb regimen for a child with T1DM should note that even a low-carb meal that includes significant protein will raise blood sugar several hours after a meal and often requires meal-time insulin to compensate.

Ketogenic Diets Are Not for Everyone

While we do advocate for ketogenic diets, we also acknowledge that there are health conditions for which they are unsuitable. The contra-indications presented below are based on information from the physician experts in the application of ketogenic diets at Johns Hopkins Hospital and are offered to help you and your physician or health care professional determine if a ketogenic diet is right for you.[39]

Contraindicated Metabolic Conditions

Individuals with these medical conditions should NOT undertake a ketogenic diet.

- Carnitine deficiency (primary)
- Carnitine palmitoyltransferase (CPT) I or II deficiency
- Carnitine translocase deficiency
- Beta-oxidation defects
- Medium-chain acyl dehydrogenase deficiency (MCAD)
- Long-chain acyl dehydrogenase deficiency (LCAD)
- Short-chain acyl dehydrogenase deficiency (SCAD)
- Long-chain 3-hydroxyacyl-CoA deficiency
- Medium-chain 3-hydroxyacyl-CoA deficiency
- Pyruvate carboxylase deficiency
- Porphyria

Note that most of these conditions are identified early in life although porphyria can develop at any time.

Health Conditions That May be Incompatible

Talk to your doctor about implementing a ketogenic diet if you have any of the following conditions. Additional health monitoring by your physician may be needed.

- History of pancreatitis
- Active gall bladder disease
- Impaired liver function
- Impaired fat digestion
- Poor nutritional status
- Gastric bypass surgery
- Decreased gastrointestinal motility
- Advanced chronic kidney disease
- Pregnancy and lactation

Part 2

The Ketogenic Diet in Action

3

Getting Ready to Start

For the past forty to fifty years, physicians and dietitians alike have been taught that a high-carbohydrate diet is best, not only for all Americans over the age of two, but also for those with diabetes. When compared to either dietary protein or fat, carbohydrate, especially refined starch and sugar, requires large amounts of insulin to move the glucose it produces into cells to be metabolized for energy or stored as fat. Thus, of all the macronutrients, carbohydrate places the greatest demand on the pancreatic beta cells. Since carbohydrate is a nonessential macronutrient, and since diabetes is a state of carbohydrate intolerance by virtue of the impaired ability to make, secrete, or remain sensitive to insulin, it makes common sense that carbohydrate would be the macronutrient to minimize.

The ketogenic diet may seem extreme to some, but not to Hippocrates who said, "Extreme remedies are very appropriate for extreme diseases."

You might ask, "Why not just cut out the refined starches and sugar?" Well, that would be a great first step and may be all that is necessary for those with mild glucose intolerance. But as we will see, for most people with diabetes, it may not be enough to lower blood glucose toward normal and protect against the damage of hyperglycemia.

The ketogenic diet that we present in this book emphasizes nutrient-dense, whole foods rich in natural fats and complete proteins, while restricting all foods high in carbohydrates. Once the total carbohydrate load is restricted, blood glucose and insulin requirements come down, stored fat can be accessed and used for fuel, and appetite is controlled by virtue of having restored cellular-fuel utilization. In other words, once your cells' ability to sense energy availability returns to normal, hunger takes care of itself. That's why calorie restriction is not the primary focus of a ketogenic diet.

For those needing to shed excess fat, it is particularly important to mind the appetite signals. Avoid eating out of habit, as an activity, for emotional reasons, or when you are not hungry. In other words, a ketogenic diet won't cure a behavioral or emotional problem, but it will address the abnormal physiology that results from a high-carbohydrate diet.

Goals, Monitoring, and Side Effects

We want you to be successful on the diet, and there are two goals that we think are important to achieve. But before we discuss these goals, we want to reiterate that when you are ready to implement the diet, arrangements should be made to have a health care professional available to monitor your individual progress. Ketogenic diets have very powerful metabolic effects, and medications will need to be reduced from the start.

The first goal is to reduce blood sugar and insulin needs and increase ketone levels. Meeting this goal is based on an effective use of protein moderation, carbohydrate restriction, and, if needed, an adjustment in meal size to minimize "after meal" blood-sugar spikes and associated insulin needs that can derail blood-sugar control. The ketogenic diet is an excellent tool for this purpose because high-fat foods and the right amount of protein are satisfying and have the metabolic effect of reducing hunger.

The second goal is to treat possible side effects associated with starting the diet. Treating side effects includes management of medications and supplements to support dietary goals and changes to insulin dosing as the diet progresses. *We implore you: pay attention to this goal and our warning!* Again, this diet is very powerful, and insulin dosages will typically need to be reduced from the start of the diet. The same goes for other medications, such as those for lowering blood pressure. Please work with your physician to address your medication changes before starting the diet.

Goal #1: Lower Blood Sugar, Increase Ketones

Your task in adhering to a ketogenic diet is to achieve a state of nutritional ketosis by significantly reducing carbohydrate intake and eating adequate but not excessive amounts of protein. For most people, eating excessive amounts of protein and/or carbohydrate on a daily basis will stop the process of ketogenesis and halt nutritional ketosis. In response, ketone levels in the blood will fall below that which can be used efficiently by the brain. It may take between one and two weeks of strict compliance to the ketogenic diet for your ketone levels to rise above 0.5 mM. Cheating during this time will have the effect of setting you back to square one. For this reason, it is strongly recommended that you track food and supplement intake in a food log or journal, or use a food-tracking website such as fitday.com, myfitnesspal.com, or cronometer.com.

A simple food log can be kept in a ruled notebook, or you can download a log sheet which is located at the bottom of the About This Site/Resources page of the ketogenic-diet-resource.com website. Record your blood sugars and note the date, meal time, and what you ate. This information will help you determine what foods have negative effects on your blood-sugar control. Ketones can also be measured and recorded as a secondary data point.

Gather Data to Track Progress

Tracking your progress on a ketogenic diet involves three basic activities. First, have baseline laboratory blood tests performed before starting the diet and then repeat these tests periodically for comparison. Second, monitor your blood-sugar and ketone levels to determine how your food and supplement choices affect them, and third, make adjustments and troubleshoot.

Keeping a food and supplement log and recording blood-sugar readings on a consistent basis are absolute musts. Checking blood-ketone levels periodically can help ensure that carbohydrate and protein restrictions are adequate. There is just no other way to clearly understand how your food choices affect blood-sugar and ketone values without tracking what and how much you eat and what supplements you take. The other benefit of logging food, supplements, and blood measurements is having this information available to share with your health care professional.

Laboratory Tests

Most health practitioners will want to see the results of your laboratory tests as they work with you on the diet. In addition to the standard diabetes blood tests (HbA1c, fructosamine), a complete blood count and a blood chemistry panel are helpful to check for kidney and anemia issues. A lipid panel is used to check cholesterol and triglyceride levels, and you may also want to have your iron, magnesium, and vitamin D levels checked. Some practitioners may also want to see a Vitamin B12 test, and tests for inflammation may also be requested. These may include a high-sensitivity C-reactive protein (hs-CRP) test and other marker tests for oxidative stress, a potent driver of inflammation. It is again strongly recommended that you find a qualified health care practitioner to monitor your progress.

Tools for Measuring Glucose and Ketone Levels

Accurate blood-sugar and ketone measurements are an important part of managing T1DM with a ketogenic diet. At this time of publication, there are two blood-sugar meters found to be highly accurate in published studies: the Freestyle Lite and the Freestyle Freedom Lite blood-sugar meters from Abbott Laboratories. Other meters that did well in testing include the AccuCheck Aviva Plus and the AccuCheck Go.[40]

Currently, there are three ways to test for ketones: urine tests, home blood meters, and the newest method—using a breath ketone analyzer called Ketonix. Urine-ketone strips are the least expensive option and are available in most pharmacies. They are the best option when first beginning a ketogenic diet. In a minority of individuals, urine ketones can decrease due an improvement in the kidney's ability to retain ketones which results in low or negative urine ketones despite the presence of nutritional ketosis. The Precision Xtra blood-ketone meter by Abbott Laboratories and test strips are more expensive but measure blood beta-hydroxybutyrate levels quite accurately. The Ketonix breath acetone meter is a one-time expense, making it quite cost effective. Ketonix is also easy and convenient to use. It has not been independently tested against blood or urine measurements, so each individual needs to make one's own correlation between its percentage readout and one's personal therapeutic goals.

We'll talk about measuring blood sugar and ketones in conjunction with a ketogenic diet in greater detail in chapter 8.

Goal #2: Treat Possible Side Effects

Since the ketogenic diet is metabolically powerful, it does come with some potential side effects. As mentioned previously, medication and insulin dosages will most likely have to be reduced immediately. In addition, while it's unlikely that you or any other person on the diet will experience all of the known side effects, they should be discussed because they can be alarming if you don't know about them. Most of these effects are the result of not getting enough salt and other minerals, and they resolve themselves as the body adapts to the diet. Nevertheless, since they are unpleasant, let's discuss them and review methods for minimizing them.

Possible Side Effect 1: Hypoglycemia (Low Blood Glucose)

As carbohydrate intake is lowered, the meal-time insulin dose will need to be decreased. As mentioned previously, you should work with your physician to help adjust your meal-time insulin dosages. Sometimes, basal insulin doses may need to be adjusted as well. Not making these adjustments can result in hypoglycemia, which can be treated by taking one or two glucose tablets (each containing 4 grams of glucose). It may help to reduce carbohydrate levels in stages over several weeks until you can stay at lower carb levels without a reaction.

Possible Side Effect 2: Hunger and Cravings

Hunger and cravings are normal and are usually one of the most difficult challenges for those new to the diet. Over time, being "in ketosis" and adapting to this shift in metabolism have a pronounced dampening effect on hunger. This is not to say that psychological cravings will also disappear, but the biochemical drivers will be greatly reduced.

If hunger is still a problem after two to three weeks on the diet, you may be eating too many carbs or too much protein for your individual needs. Review what you're eating from your food log to be sure that your food intake matches your recommended level of macronutrients (see chapter 5). Eating one or two spoonfuls of coconut oil may also increase ketosis and help quell hunger until you get "over the hump."

If you find that you are eating the correct amounts of protein and carbohydrate, recalculate your protein grams for a higher goal weight, and see if the extra protein helps quell hunger. If so, you may be shooting for a goal weight that is too low.

Possible Side Effect 3: Weakness, Dizziness, and Fatigue Due to Dehydration

Fatigue, dizziness, and feelings of weakness or shakiness can be caused by dehydration and mineral loss. Implementing a ketogenic diet usually causes the body to rid itself of excess water and salt due to the effect of lower insulin levels on kidney function. This results in increased urination and loss of electrolytes and minerals such as sodium, potassium, calcium and magnesium in the urine.

It is the loss of these minerals and water that can result in fatigue and other symptoms of dehydration: increased thirst, dry mouth, cramping, weakness, irritability, headache, dizziness, palpitations, sluggishness, and fainting. Replace the minerals and fluids by sipping meat and chicken broth and eating more green leafy vegetables. You can also drink a cup or two of homemade mineral water from the recipe in appendix A or use salt substitutes containing potassium to replace lost salt and potassium. (Warning: if you're taking diuretics or have been advised by your physician to avoid salt, work with your doctor to implement this diet before changing your salt or potassium intake.) You may want to take a mineral supplement:

> Take magnesium citrate supplements as recommended in appendix A. (If there are kidney issues in your medical history, don't take oral magnesium or potassium supplements without checking with the physician responsible for the care of those conditions.)

> To keep sodium levels up, don't be afraid to add salt to meals. If you experience weakness or a "woozy" or "unfocused" feeling, you can add salt by either by putting one quarter teaspoon of sea salt in a glass of water and drinking it or by having a cup or two of the homemade mineral water solution in appendix A. Symptoms should improve shortly if a mineral imbalance is the problem.

> To keep potassium levels up, eat more avocado and green leafy vegetables.

Possible Side Effect 4: Constipation or Diarrhea

Constipation can be an indication of low magnesium, a side effect of pain drugs, and/or the result of dehydration. Individuals with slow gastrointestinal (GI) motility (due to drugs or disease) should discuss options to address constipation with their physician. There are products recommended for constipation such as Milk of Magnesia, MiraLax, or Movicol (Polyethylene Glycol 3350) and stool softeners such as Dulcolax. Laxative teas are another option. Examples include Smooth Move from Traditional Medicinals and Get Regular from Yogi brand.

Bulky greens such as romaine lettuce and sautéed mixed greens can also ease constipation. Fiber-bulking products such as psyllium husk powder should not be used if you are currently constipated, but can be used after bowel movements return to normal. (See the Dietary Fiber section in chapter 4 for details.) Individuals with ulcerative colitis, Crohn's disease, or bowel obstruction issues should not use psyllium husk. Talk to your doctor about other options, especially if you have any medical conditions.

Although constipation is more common, some people experience diarrhea the first week or two of a ketogenic diet. We believe this may be associated with either a reaction of the gut microbiota to a change in food choices, or excessive magnesium or coconut oil intake. If it is a gut microbiota reaction, it should clear up in a few days.

Possible Side Effect 5: Muscle Cramps

Muscle cramps may result from water and mineral losses as discussed in Possible Side Effect 3. Dosages of diuretic drugs may need to be adjusted as ketogenic diets are naturally diuretic. It's important to discuss this first with your prescribing physician before making changes. For muscle cramps, drink more water and follow the recommendations of Dr. Jeff Volek and Dr. Stephen Phinney in their book *The Art and Science of Low Carbohydrate Living*. They recommend taking three slow-release magnesium tablets each day (e.g., Slow-Mag or Mag 64) for twenty days and then continuing to take one tablet a day thereafter to prevent muscle cramps. (Again, individuals with kidney problems should not take oral magnesium or potassium supplements without checking with the physician responsible for treating those conditions.)

Possible Side Effect 6: Ketone Breath

Excess ketones can be expelled from the body via the lungs and in the urine. The main ketone in breath is acetone, which has a distinctive smell. Ketone breath is described as being "fruity" or "metallic." As your body adapts to using the ketones as fuel, less should be expelled in your breath. Although ketone breath may be noticed by significant others, we consider it a good indicator that you've achieved the state of nutritional ketosis. Non-sugar-containing breath mints or mouthwash will effectively disguise the mild odor of acetone.

Possible Side Effect 7: Weight Changes

A ketogenic diet lowers blood glucose, which lowers insulin needs and may eventually lower caloric intake as hunger subsides. If you experience unintended weight loss, eat more calories in the form of natural fats (butter, macadamia nuts, and avocados) on a daily basis until the weight loss stops. If this doesn't help, add an ounce or two of protein to your daily totals.

Possible Side Effect 8: Changes in Blood Pressure

High insulin levels result in greater retention of salt and water. For some people, this excess water storage translates into high blood pressure. Once insulin requirements decrease, the kidneys excrete excess water. Blood pressure should drop as a result. For this reason, a physician should monitor all blood pressure medication being taken. If you take blood pressure medication, you may find that you become lightheaded and dizzy after a week on the diet. This is a sign that you may need to reduce your blood pressure medication dose.

Possible Side Effect 9: Vitamin and Mineral Deficiencies

Vitamin and mineral supplementation is recommended since certain food groups are restricted. However, there is no need to take mega doses of vitamins. A basic multivitamin/multi-mineral supplement that contains the RDA (recommended daily allowance) for all vitamins and minerals is a good start. Pay particular attention that the multivitamin contains the RDA for zinc and selenium. Appendix A lists supplement recommendations.

Possible Side Effect 10: Heart Palpitations or a "Racing" Heart

Some people may experience heart palpitations or a racing heart when starting a ketogenic diet. It's been reported that this is more likely if the person normally has low blood pressure. There are several factors that may be involved in this symptom.

> First, there may be nutrient deficiencies. This is why a multivitamin containing the RDA for selenium and zinc, plus a magnesium supplement, broth, or mineral water are strongly recommended.

> Second, there may be an electrolyte imbalance, or you may be dehydrated. Making some homemade mineral water and drinking a cup with your morning and evening meal should help if this is the issue. (See Possible Side Effect 3.) In addition, drink plenty of water.

> Third, some people may have "racing" heart reactions to excessive coconut oil or medium chain triglyceride (MCT) oil consumption. If you add these oils to your diet, start with small amounts and increase over time. Don't rely on coconut or MCT oil for your only fat intake. Be sure to include other fats such as butter, ghee, olive oil, and animal fats as well.

> Finally, this symptom may be associated with hypoglycemic reactions as discussed in Possible Side Effect 1. Treat it with several glucose tablets as you would normally for hypoglycemia.

Possible Side Effect 11: Nausea

Many people are not used to eating the amount of fat allowed on a ketogenic diet. Nausea is common after eating a high-fat meal or a after taking coconut oil or MCT oil. If this happens, try decreasing fat intake and slowly increasing it over time or spreading out your fat intake over smaller meals and snacks.

Final Note on Side Effects and Broth

Many side effects can be managed just by making sure your electrolyte and mineral intake is adequate. Bone and meat broths are a great way to do this. Look for organic chicken, beef, and vegetable broths without MSG (monosodium glutamate) or make your own broth. You can find many recipes on the Internet with a quick search.

Concerns about Elevated Cholesterol

Many people have trouble on a ketogenic diet plan because they are alarmed about increasing the amount of fat they eat, especially saturated fat. This becomes an issue particularly if their total-cholesterol levels go up and their physicians voice concerns about higher cholesterol levels.

A physician's concern is understandable. The message that eating fat and cholesterol is harmful has been pounded into the collective American psyche for the last forty years. It's also difficult to unlearn the message that high cholesterol is the cause of heart disease. Yes, these messages have been repeated over and over, but they are both untrue. Dr. Ron Rosedale, an expert on ketogenic diets, writes about this myth, and there are several good books on this subject.[41] Nina Teicholz's *The Big Fat Surprise* is one such book. There's also an excellent article titled "Cholesterol: Friend or Foe" written by Dr. Natasha Campbell McBride.[42]

The real culprit of atherosclerosis is chronically elevated blood glucose and insulin, and the associated inflammatory damage to artery walls. Cholesterol is used to repair this arterial damage, not cause it. Hyperglycemia and hyperinsulinemia are why diabetics and those with metabolic syndrome suffer from higher rates of heart disease. For most people, following a ketogenic diet over time improves the risk markers for cardiovascular health.

Fifteen Tips for Success

Here are additional tips and techniques for maximizing your success on the diet.

1. You must keep track of what you eat on a per-meal basis, at least at the beginning. Both carbohydrates and proteins must be tracked so as not to go over the daily recommended amount. Keep a spreadsheet, use a web-based food-intake tracker, or keep a written food log or journal. Journaling will help you accurately record food intake, and it can also be used to track mood and physical changes for analysis should there be a need to troubleshoot.

2. Recommended tools include Fitday, which offers both a web-based application and an application that can be downloaded to a PC. MyFitnessPal is another good choice, and it's free, as are FatSecret, Cronometer, and the USDA's nutrition database. Finally, the Atkins website also has some nice tools for tracking progress.

3. Get a carbohydrate-counting guidebook or a software application for counting carbohydrates in various foods. Counting carbohydrates is a crucial part of the diet, so it's important to understand how to do this correctly and accurately.

4. Purchase a good quality digital food scale. It should be accurate to at least one gram. This ensures accurate tracking of food amounts and calories.

5. Go on a carbohydrate sweep. Inspect your kitchen cupboards and refrigerator, removing or separating all high-carbohydrate foods. Restock or rearrange the kitchen so that low-carb, ketogenic foods

are readily available. A low-carbohydrate food list is included in the Foods to Eat section in chapter 4.

6. Recognize that a ketogenic diet plan is not a "special diet" that requires special foods. Ketogenic foods are essentially real, whole foods close to their natural state. Avoid low-carbohydrate "convenience foods" such as shakes and bars. They are typically loaded with poor-quality proteins and sugar alcohols that are not healthy and can affect blood-glucose levels.

7. Be prepared to spend more time in the kitchen. This is an important point. A ketogenic diet involves cooking and eating real foods. If you are unable to cook for yourself, check in with your local grocery store and stock up on whole, simple, cooked foods such as roasted chicken and steamed seafood.

8. Think about meal logistics, and learn to plan accordingly. This will help provide a framework to follow, starting with buying the right food at the grocery store. If proper foods have already been selected for dinner, it's easier to avoid making poor selections based on old habits.

9. Replace old habits with new ones. If the normal routine is to visit the nearest coffee shop for a bagel, start making coffee at home and have it with eggs instead.

10. Don't let travel situations put you in a bind. With low-carbohydrate diets increasing in popularity, you can find suitable options almost anywhere in a pinch. Most gas station convenience stores now carry nuts, cheese, beef jerky, and hard-boiled eggs. See the Travel Tips section in chapter 6 for more information.

11. Stay hydrated. As carbohydrate intake is lowered, your kidneys will start dumping excess water. At the very least, make sure to drink enough water to replace what is lost. A good general rule is to drink half the number of pounds of your goal body weight in ounces of water each day. Broths without MSG are good choices for hydration because they also provide minerals.

12. Think about any social situations that will be encountered. Devise ways to handle temptations to eat the "old" way. This will help with being blindsided when someone at the office brings in a box of cookies. Likewise, a beer with friends usually turns into a date with potato skins and nachos. Think salad and steak instead.

13. Talk with household members. Let them and others know that certain foods are required for adherence to the diet. It is more difficult to follow the diet if someone else in the house has eaten the dinner you had prepared.

14. Monitor your progress. There's nothing like seeing your blood sugar come down—and stay down—to help with motivation.

15. Don't be afraid to eat more fat. Many people have trouble on a ketogenic diet because they just can't get past the idea that eating lots of fat is bad, especially saturated animal fat.

In the next chapter, we will provide detailed information about the right types of fats and other macronutrients to choose, and what you should and should not eat on a ketogenic diet.

4

Food Facts and What to Eat

Now, let's move onto some general concepts regarding foods you will consume on a ketogenic diet. Remember, there are three main macronutrients: fat, protein, and carbohydrate. There are details about various choices within these macronutrient categories that are important for you to know for success, so let's go over them.

About Dietary Fats

Let's talk about fats first because they constitute the majority of calories you'll consume on the diet. There are several types of fats and oils that have different effects on the body. They fall into three major groups according to their chemical structure. These include saturated fats, monounsaturated fats, and polyunsaturated fats.

- *Saturated fats (SFA)* are solid at room temperature, like lard, butter, and coconut oil. These fats are most stable chemically and the least inflammatory.

- *Monounsaturated fats (MUFA)* are liquid at room temperature and somewhat stable chemically. These include beef tallow and olive, avocado, macadamia, and hazelnut oils.

- *Polyunsaturated fats (PUFA)* are the least stable of all the fats, since they are prone to rancidity when affected by heat and light. There are two types: omega-6 and omega-3. Omega-6 fats in particular tend to be inflammatory to the body. Somewhat less inflammatory are the now famous omega-3 fats found in fish oil and fatty fish.

Since dietary fats will be a prominent part of your daily meals, they should be chosen with digestive tolerance in mind. Saturated and monounsaturated fats such as butter, macadamia nuts, coconut oil, olive oil, avocado, and egg yolks are tolerated more easily as most people cannot handle eating large amounts of polyunsaturated fats. Examples of omega-6 PUFA include vegetable oils such as soybean, sunflower, safflower, corn, and canola, plus products containing these oils such as mayonnaise and margarine.

Your intake of PUFA from vegetable oils should be minimized. Most nuts and seeds (with the exception of macadamias) are high in omega-6 fatty acids, but they contain many other micronutrients and their omega-6 content may not be problematic.[43] Omega-3 fats can be found in fatty fish such as anchovies, sardines, salmon, tuna, and grass-fed meats. A good rule of thumb is to emphasize fish and grass-fed meat in your meals, limit nuts to a few ounces each day, and avoid vegetable oils as much as possible.

Natural Fats versus Trans Fats

Contrary to popular rhetoric, natural fats and cholesterol from animal foods and tropical fats from coconut and palm seeds are nourishing and should never have been disparaged or limited in our diets. In addition to the vegetable-oil fats mentioned above, "bad" fats also include the trans fats, which are manmade products associated with hydrogenating commercial seed oils (e.g., Crisco), and which are included in many processed foods as a substitute for saturated fats. To avoid these fats, avoid foods with the word "hydrogenated" in the ingredients listed on the label. Many studies that originally implicated naturally occurring saturated fats in heart disease looked at them in combination with trans fats, and it was actually the trans fats that had harmful effects on cardiovascular health. When studied in the absence of manmade trans fats, naturally saturated fats do not contribute to heart disease.

Trans fats are finally being phased out of our food supply. This is good news because trans fats worsen the risk of heart disease by lowering HDL cholesterol and increasing LDL cholesterol along with another heart-disease risk marker called Lp(a) or lipoprotein(a), a subclass of LDL cholesterol. Trans fats are also associated with an increased risk for stroke and type 2 diabetes. The best way to avoid trans fats is to avoid processed foods altogether.

Coconut Oil and MCTs

Coconut oil is a source of fat on a ketogenic diet that has some special properties. In addition to being a source of long-chain fatty acids, it also contains natural medium-chain triglycerides (MCTs). MCTs have a chemical structure that allows them to bypass normal fatty acid digestion pathways. Instead of being packaged up to travel through the blood, MCTs are passed directly from the intestinal tract to the liver. In addition, MCTs are not stored in fat cells, so they must be burned for energy or converted into ketones by the liver.

The addition of small amounts of coconut oil to your diet will help elevate ketones quickly. However, coconut oil or MCTs can cause diarrhea if over consumed. And, despite the fact that MCTs cannot be stored in fat cells, when consumed in excess, the calories from them can quickly add up and divert other excess calories to be stored in fat cells, contributing to obesity. In other words, if your goal is to lose weight, MCTs will have to be processed before body fat can be burned.

Organic coconut oil is much more available now than it used to be. There are many different brands, and you can buy it online or at your local grocery store or natural food store. Unrefined coconut oil has a strong flavor and odor of coconut. If you prefer a milder flavor, but still wish to experience the benefits of including this MCT-rich oil in your diet, look for "refined" coconut oil.

About Protein

Foods that contain protein are the source of the amino acids needed to create and maintain body proteins. There are nine essential amino acids that our bodies can't create from other nutrients, so they must be obtained from our diet. The daily requirement for protein intake ranges from a minimum amount needed to maintain current function to an optimal amount that allows for muscle growth and repair to support exercise and fitness. For most people on a ketogenic diet, protein intake should range from 1 to 1.5 grams/kg of goal body weight per day. Consider that range to be a starting point to be adjusted based on your individual needs.

In general, animal proteins are referred to as complete proteins because they have all of the essential and nonessential proteins in the proper ratios that humans need. Vegetables, fruits, and legumes have less protein and more carbohydrate per serving when compared to animal sources. Additionally, plant proteins are often incomplete: they may lack or have smaller amounts of one or more of the essential amino acids.

Protein plays a role in just about every metabolic process in the human body and is required for retaining lean muscle tissue when carbohydrate intake is restricted. It also helps reduce hunger, so make sure you consume protein with each meal. However, don't go overboard. Excessive protein intake necessitates a higher insulin dose than would otherwise be required to control blood sugar. The extra insulin needed to process excessive protein intake also inhibits ketone formation in the liver: not a desired outcome in the treatment of diabetes with a ketogenic diet.

Choosing protein sources that are higher in fat will allow you to have larger servings and still stay within your protein limits. For instance, if you plan to have 28 grams of protein at your meal, a serving of a fatty meat like 80% lean ground beef will be more satisfying than a portion of lean chicken breast because the beef will contain more fat along with the protein. The same goes for a serving of country-style pork ribs instead of shrimp, or a salmon fillet instead of a turkey breast. Go for the dark meat, high-fat choice when you can. The food lists in appendix C provide protein grams and fat grams so you can easily see which protein choices contain more fat.

About Carbohydrates

A quote from the *Principles of Biochemistry by* Albert Lehninger explains in simple terms, one of the reasons why carbohydrates compose 45% to 65% of calories in a standard American diet. Mr. Lehninger wrote:

> *"Carbohydrates per se are not essential in the human diet,*
> *but because carbohydrate-rich foods are abundant and*
> *cheap compared with fats and protein, they naturally form*
> *a major part of the diet in most of the world".*

Dietary carbohydrates include foods containing sugars such as glucose, fructose, lactose, and sucrose. Carbohydrates also include starches, such as those found in potatoes, winter squashes, wheat flour, oats, beans, rice, peas, and similar foods.

Dietary fiber is the indigestible carbohydrate part of plant foods. Its presence can delay glucose absorption and gastric emptying, which blunt blood-sugar response to the food. Of course, limiting sugar and starch intake on a ketogenic diet has an even more potent effect on blunting blood-sugar spikes. This is the reason that non-starchy green vegetables—which contain plenty of dietary fiber, vitamins, minerals, potassium, and antioxidants—make up the majority of vegetable choices on a ketogenic diet. Dietary fiber is also fuel for healthy gut bacteria. Gut bacteria consume the fiber and make short-chain fatty acids, which supply an important fuel to cells lining your colon.

Keep in mind that all the carbohydrate our bodies need can be created internally without difficulty. The vast majority of available dietary carbohydrates are not essential to good health. Evolutionary biology teaches us that for 99.9% of human existence, carbohydrates were a small or inconsistent component of our diet.[44] This lesson is especially valuable for those with diabetes.

Remember that diabetes is a state of profound carbohydrate intolerance. It is a simple fact that the more dietary carbohydrate you consume, the more difficult it will be to control your blood sugar.

A study by Boden et al. at Temple University School of Medicine in Philadelphia showed how carbohydrate consumption affects blood-sugar control. Boden's team followed ten obese subjects with T2DM. For the first few weeks they ate a diet which included 300 grams of carbohydrate each day. During the second phase of the study, the subjects ate only 20 grams of carbohydrate per day. After only two weeks on a low-carbohydrate ketogenic diet containing 20 grams of carbohydrate per day, the blood sugar and insulin responses of the subjects were greatly reduced compared to the levels resulting from the diet containing 300 grams of carbohydrate per day.[45] The authors estimated that if the group had remained on the low-carb diet for eight weeks (the minimum time required for an HbA1c test to reflect the new state of lower blood sugar), the average HbA1c would have decreased from 7.3% to 5.6%.

Consuming refined carbohydrates (e.g., high-fructose corn syrup, fructose, and sucrose) in significant quantities is detrimental to human health. The adverse effects of refined-carbohydrate consumption are even more serious for persons with diabetes. We can't stress this enough, and we strongly encourage people with diabetes to avoid foods containing refined sugars.

Watch Food Labels for Hidden Carbohydrates

Sugars, starches, and sugar alcohols are hidden in all kinds of processed foods and are listed under many different names. Be diligent about reading labels to find hidden carbohydrates. You may recognize some of these common names.

- *Sugars:* glucose, fructose, sucrose, honey, brown sugar, brown rice syrup, beet sugar, coconut sugar, dextrose, molasses, corn sugar, corn syrup, high-fructose corn syrup, fruit-juice concentrate, cane juice, treacle, lactose, galactose, maltose, maltodextrin, hydro-lyzed starch, demerara, turbinado, maple syrup, and agave syrup.

- *Starches*: corn starch, vegetable starch, arrowroot, cassava, ama-ranth, barley, wheat, wheat starch, buckwheat, corn, HVP, HPP, malt, millet, modified food starch, oats, potato, quinoa, rice, sorghum, spelt, teff, tapioca, and triticale.

- *Sugar alcohols*: polydextrose, glycerin, maltitol, mannitol, sor-bitol, xylitol, erythritol, glycerol, isomalt, lactitol, and inositol.

Generally, any chemical name with an *ose* ending is a sugar, and any chemical name ending with an *ol* is a sugar alcohol.

Don't rely on food labels to give you accurate carb counts. Food manufacturers naturally have an interest in underreporting carbohydrate amounts in their products. The USDA nutrition database is a better source for the actual carbohydrate content of foods. Remember to check serving sizes as well. When looking at a large container of yogurt that has 16 grams of carbohydrate per serving, verify the number of servings in the container. If there are two servings, then the total carbohydrate count for that container is 32 grams, not 16 grams.

Dietary Fiber

Dietary fiber is the indigestible carbohydrate part of plant foods. Its presence can delay glucose absorption and gastric emptying, which blunts blood sugar response to the food. Dietary fiber is also a food source for your healthy gut bacteria. A byproduct of their consumption of the fiber is a short-chain fatty acid called butyrate. Butyrate has many beneficial effects for the cells lining the wall of your colon. Not only is it a source of energy, but butyrate has anti-inflammatory effects.[46] Ketogenic diets can be low in fiber if you don't eat enough green leafy vegetables. Focus on sources of soluble fiber including non-starchy vegetables, chia seeds, or ground flaxseed. Romaine lettuce can be used to add bulk fiber to the diet, as can spinach or kale.

If you prefer to take fiber separately, try a gentle, soluble fiber such as psyllium husk. Plain psyllium husk powder is recommended, since products such as Metamucil or its generic equivalents have fillers which contain carbohydrate. Keep in mind that psyllium may reduce or delay the absorption of certain medications. In addition, it is poorly fermented, meaning you'll miss out on feeding your healthy gut bacteria.[47]

As a rule, don't take psyllium supplements at the same time you take other medication or supplements. Take psyllium at least one hour before or two to four hours after taking other medications. Psyllium husk is not recommended for people with ulcerative colitis or adhesions or if you have difficulty swallowing. Also, never take psyllium if you are constipated, as it can cause an intestinal obstruction.

In any event, it's best to introduce it slowly. Begin with one half teaspoon in eight ounces of warm water once a day. Mix it well, and then drink it immediately before it becomes too thick to swallow comfortably. (Psyllium thickens rapidly when added to water.) Over time, increase the quantity until you reach the amount that works for you. Most experts recommend two teaspoons in two large glasses of water per day, as needed. Always take psyllium with a full glass of water, and drink at least six to eight glasses of water throughout the day to avoid constipation.

Water and Dehydration

Everyone needs water to replace what the body loses through daily activity. On a ketogenic diet, it is even more important, since the diet has a diuretic effect.

Drinking plenty of water also helps to remove metabolic waste from the body and supports many different metabolic functions. It's logical that water is lost when you urinate or sweat, but you may not realize that small amounts of water are lost each time you exhale. You need to replace this lost water to prevent dehydration. We can't emphasize enough how important it is that you drink plenty of water. In addition, your body will need more water if you live in a hot or dry climate, are more physically active, are sick and running a fever, or have diarrhea or are vomiting. Some people may have fluid restrictions because of health problems such as heart or kidney disease. If your health care provider has told you to restrict fluid intake, be sure to follow that advice.

Artificial Sweeteners

A recent joint statement from the American Heart Association and American Diabetes Association reviewed five nonnutritive sweeteners that had been evaluated and deemed safe as food additives by the US Food and Drug Administration. The sweeteners reviewed included aspartame, acesulfame-K, neotame, saccharin, and sucralose. The authors of the review did not further investigate the safety of nonnutritive sweeteners as that had already been done by the US Food and Drug Administration. The authors did conclude the following:

At this time, there are insufficient data to determine conclusively whether the use of nonnutritive sweeteners to displace caloric sweeteners in beverages and foods reduces added sugars or carbohydrate intakes, or benefits appetite, energy balance, body weight, or cardiometabolic risk factors.

From the experience of those following a ketogenic diet, eliminating sugar and refined carbohydrates and limiting total carbohydrates will go a long way toward resetting your taste buds so that the real sweetness in natural foods can be enjoyed. You may find that eliminating artificial sweeteners will also help you feel satisfied with the natural sweetness in foods.

Stevia has become popular recently as a natural sweetener, and some food manufacturers have begun adding it to various products. The US Food and Drug Administration has not made a determination as to the "Generally Recognized As Safe" status of stevia, but it has not issued any objection letters for a number of "Generally Recognized As Safe" notifications for stevia sweeteners. Japan and other countries have allowed the use of stevia as a food sweetener for many years and no adverse effects have been reported.

Using small amounts of stevia or sucralose occasionally should have little effect on blood sugar. Blood-sugar testing after use of these sweeteners is advised so you'll be aware of your individual reaction.

Sugar alcohols are another choice of artificial sweetener. Ellen gives the pros and cons of each type of sugar alcohol on her website.[48] Erythritol, in particular, seems to be tolerated more easily than other sugar alcohols. Other types such as maltitol can cause digestive issues when consumed in large amounts, and older studies have shown maltitol and sorbitol to be anti-ketogenic, meaning they interfere with ketosis.

Using Condiments

A majority of condiment foods contain sugar or starchy fillers. For instance, a tablespoon of regular ketchup contains nearly five grams of carbohydrate. In addition, pickles, black-bean sauce, taco sauce, sweet hot sauces, vinegar, salsa, miso, chili peppers, marinades, barbecue sauce, and soy sauce also contain significant amounts of carbohydrate. If you use these foods in more than tiny amounts, you may want to count those extra carb grams. In general, you'll find that condiments that are higher in fat will be lower in carbohydrate. Pesto, mayonnaise, and full-fat dressings that have less than one carb per serving are good choices.

Foods To Eat

The lists below will help you determine which foods to choose for success in achieving lower blood sugars.

Fats and Oils

As we discussed earlier, saturated and monounsaturated fats are healthier overall. We've marked each item below as to whether they are mostly saturated (S), monounsaturated (M), or polyunsaturated (P). Avoid hydrogenated fats, such as margarine, to minimize trans fat intake. If you use seed or vegetable oils (olive, canola, sunflower, safflower, soybean, flaxseed, and sesame oils) select "cold-pressed" organic brands and avoid heating them if possible. In addition, cold-pressed oils should be refrigerated to minimize rancidity. Some of the more unusual fats listed below can be obtained online.

- Avocado (M) (count carbs)
- Avocado oil (M)
- Almond oil (P, M)
- Beef tallow, preferably from grass-fed cattle (S, M)
- Butter (organic or Kerrygold brands) (S)
- Chicken or duck fat, organic pastured (S, M)
- Ghee (butter with milk solids removed) (S)
- Lard that is not hydrogenated (S, M)
- Macadamia nuts (M)
- Macadamia oil (M)
- Mayonnaise, no or low sugar (Duke's and Hellmann's brands are low or no sugar) (P)
- Olive oil, organic (M)
- Olives, green and black (M)
- Organic coconut oil, coconut butter, and coconut-cream concentrate (S)
- Organic red palm oil (S)
- Peanut butter (unsweetened products) and limit the amount consumed due to omega-6 content (P, M)
- Seed and most nut butters and oils (P)
- Dark chocolate, 90% cocoa (small amounts) (S, M)

Sources of Protein

While not critical to success, choosing wild-caught seafood, organic eggs, and organic or grass-fed animal foods is recommended. Websites such as www.eatwild.com or www.localharvest.org can help with locating local sources of clean, grass-fed meats and poultry.

- *Whole eggs:* these can be prepared in various ways. Try deviled, fried, hard-boiled, omelets, poached, scrambled, and soft-boiled.
- *Meat:* all cuts of beef, pork, lamb, veal, and goat. Look out for added sugar in hams and prepared deli meats. Fattier cuts of meat are better because they contain less protein and more fat.
- *Game meat:* venison, elk, buffalo/bison, and other wild game are fantastic sources of protein, although these meats are usually lower in fat than beef and pork.
- *Organ meats/offal:* organ meats such as liver and heart are extremely nutritious. Roasted marrow bones are an especially fat-rich culinary treat.
- *Poultry:* chicken, turkey, quail, Cornish hen, duck, goose, and pheasant. Free range is better, if it's available. Dark meat is better because of the higher fat content. There is no need to purchase skinless poultry. The skin is rich in fat and protein, and when roasted until crispy, it's delicious! You will also find that skin-on, bone-in poultry is more economical than boneless, skinless cuts.
- *Shellfish and seafood:* clams, crab, lobster, scallops, shrimp, squid, mussels, and oysters. (The exception is imitation crab meat; it often contains sugar and gluten.)
- *Fish of any kind:* anchovies, calamari, catfish, cod, flounder, halibut, herring, mackerel, mahi-mahi, salmon, sardines, scrod, sole, snapper, trout, and tuna. When buying canned salmon and sardines, favor varieties with the bones and skin. The bones provide minerals, and the skin provides more of the important omega-3 fats. (Exceptions include breaded and fried seafood, which are high in carbohydrates.)
- *Bacon and sausage:* check labels and avoid those cured with excessive sugar (maple flavor for example) or containing fillers such as textured vegetable protein (TVP), soy isolate, wheat gluten, or milk protein. Specialty health-food stores carry most brands of sugar-free and filler-free bacon and sausage. Each serving should have no more than one carb.

- *Peanut butter and whole soy products:* tempeh, tofu, and edamame (soybeans) are good sources of protein, but they contain carbohydrates, so track them carefully.
- *Protein powders:* whey, rice, pea, hemp, or other vegetable protein powders can be used occasionally, but read the labels for added sugars. Also, don't rely on them exclusively as a protein source.
- *Nuts and seeds:* macadamias are the highest in fat and lowest in carbohydrate. Pecans, almonds, and walnuts are good choices. Cashews are higher in carbohydrate so track intake carefully to avoid going over your limits.
- *Special note about fried pork rinds:* they have zero carbohydrate and can be used as an occasional snack; however, the protein in them does not contain all of the necessary amino acids. Count the protein grams but limit the amount so as not to displace other complete-protein foods.

Fresh Vegetables

Most non-starchy vegetables are low in carbohydrates and are good choices. You should eat at least 1 to 2 cups of green, leafy vegetables each day to obtain potassium and vitamins C, K, and E. Choose organic vegetables to avoid pesticide residues. If you choose frozen or canned products, read the labels to make sure no sugar is added. You'll note that winter squashes, potatoes, sweet potatoes and yams, peas, dried beans, corn, and other starchy choices aren't shown in the following list. These vegetables are high in carbohydrate, so it's best to limit or avoid them.

In addition, you'll see an asterisk (*) next to the sweeter vegetables, such as onions, shallots, tomatoes, carrots, peppers, and summer squashes. These should be limited, as they are relatively high in carbohydrate, and even small amounts can add up quickly. This list is by no means exhaustive, so if you have other favorites and they fit within your carbohydrate limits, please enjoy them.

- Alfalfa sprouts
- Asparagus
- Avocado
- Bamboo shoots
- Bean sprouts
- Bell peppers*
- Bok choy
- Broccoli
- Brussels sprouts
- Cabbage
- Carrots*
- Cauliflower
- Celery
- Celery root
- Chives
- Cucumbers
- Dandelion greens
- Eggplant
- Fennel
- Garlic
- Green vegetable leaves (beet, collard, amaranth, turnip, and mustard)
- Green beans*
- Kale
- Kohlrabi
- Leeks
- Lettuces and salad greens (arugula, Boston lettuce, green leaf, chicory, endive, escarole, fennel, mâche, radicchio, romaine, sorrel, watercress)
- Mushrooms
- Olives
- Onions*
- Peppers, hot
- Radishes
- Scallions
- Shallots*
- Snow peas*
- Spaghetti squash
- Spinach
- Sprouts
- Summer squash*
- Swiss chard
- Tomatoes*
- Turnips and turnip greens

Dairy Products

Organic products from grass-fed animals are good choices. Limit cheese to four ounces and cream to one to two tablespoons if you want to stay under 20 grams of carbs per day.

- Full-fat sour cream (check labels for additives and fillers. Look for brands such as Daisy that are pure cream with no added milk or whey—carbohydrates and protein will be low in these products).
- Butter or ghee (organic or Kerrygold brand).
- Organic cream cheese (look for brands without added whey).
- Heavy whipping cream (at least 36% milk-fat content)
- Mascarpone cheese.
- Full-fat Greek yogurt (unsweetened).
- Full-fat cheeses (brie, cheddar, Swiss, colby).

Note that even full-fat dairy products can cause blood-sugar elevations in some people. If you find you are having trouble achieving the blood-sugar reductions you want to see, try reducing dairy products in your diet to see if you get more favorable blood-test results.

Beverages (All Unsweetened)

Beverages should be unsweetened and decaffeinated. Caffeine is restricted because it can increase blood sugar.

- Water, either plain or with lemon or lime juice in small amounts
- Clear broth, bone broth, or bouillon (no added MSG)
- Coffee
- Black or green tea, or other herbal tea
- Flavored seltzer water
- Almond milk or other nut milks (less than 2 g carb/serving)
- Soy milk (count carbohydrates and protein grams)
- Coconut milk, full-fat canned or the refrigerated carton

Spices

Spices have carbs, so you should count them if you add more than one half of a teaspoon to your meal. Also, read labels on commercial spice mixes, like steak seasoning or Greek seasoning. They usually have added sugar, as do flavored extracts. Some don't, so check labels before you buy. See appendix C for a list of spice carb counts.

Foods to Avoid

The foods below are to be avoided on a ketogenic diet, as consuming them will quickly increase blood sugar and interfere with ketosis.

Sugars and Sweetened Foods

Sugar is ever-present in our food supply and not only in candy, soft drinks, and fruit spreads. The only way to truly avoid it is to eat only fresh, unprocessed foods such as meats, poultry, seafood, eggs, nuts, and green leafy vegetables. If packaged foods are consumed, read the food labels carefully. Avoid any foods that have been sweetened with these ingredients:

- Sugars, such as white sugar (sucrose), brown sugar, cane sugar, powdered sugar, maltose, fructose, glucose, lactose and crystalline fructose
- Syrups, such as corn syrup, sorghum, honey, maple syrup, agave, evaporated cane juice or cane syrup

It makes sense to bypass the obvious sweet foods like cakes, cookies, muffins, and pies, but also look out for foods such as ketchup, soup, bread, and even canned vegetables. Sugar is added to most of these processed canned, frozen, and dried foods.

Processed and Convenience Foods

It's well known that processed foods, especially convenience foods, contain plenty of chemical preservatives, MSG, hidden sugars, and starchy additives. Here are some common examples of these types of foods:

- Chips made from potatoes or other starchy vegetables (this includes Terra chips, vegetable chips, crunchy bean pods, and the like).
- Canned soups and stews (most canned products contain hidden starchy thickeners).

- Bagged and boxed processed foods such as Hamburger Helper, stuffing mixes, puddings, and Jello gelatin. (Most are high in wheat or sugar and contain added chemicals in the form of preservatives and fillers.)

All Grains and Grain Products

Wheat flour is widely used as a filler in processed foods. Read food labels carefully and avoid or minimize any foods that contain grains. Here are some examples of what to avoid:

- Wheat, barley, rye, sorghum, triticale, teff, spelt, rice, vegetable protein, amaranth, buckwheat, millet, quinoa, corn
- Products made from grain flours, such as white flour, whole wheat flour, bread flour, oat flour, teff flour, rice flour, soy flour, breads of all kinds, waffles, pancakes, pasta, muffins, cold cereals, hot cereals, bread crumbs, tortillas, crackers, cookies, cakes, pies, pretzels, wraps, and flatbreads
- Corn products, such as cornbread, tamales, corn chips, grits, polenta, popcorn, stuffing mixes, and cornmeal (corn is in most processed foods as high-fructose corn syrup, as a thickener, or as a preservative.)
- Packaged meats and seafood breaded in any kind of grain flour or containing breadcrumbs as filler, such as prepared meatballs, fish sticks, and chicken nuggets or chicken tenders.

Starchy Vegetables

Although they can be rich in vitamins and minerals, these popular starchy foods are restricted because they can raise blood sugar very high, and very quickly. The fiber in legumes helps slow this, but they are still high in carbohydrate.

- Potatoes, sweet potatoes, yams, and potato products such as hash browns, potato chips, tater tots, and French fries.

- Corn, corn mixtures, beets, okra, acorn and butternut squash, yucca, and artichokes.
- Legumes, including most members of the bean and pea families, such as lentils, lima beans, kidney beans, and black-eyed peas.

Fruit and Fruit Products

While they do have some health benefits, fruits in any form (dried, fresh, or frozen) are high in carbohydrates and fructose. Fructose, even from natural fruit, places a metabolic load on the liver and can drive up blood sugar if eaten in large amounts.

- Bananas, grapes, oranges, peaches, and dried fruit are the highest in carbohydrate. Avoid them, as they will sharply increase blood sugar.
- Berries are the lowest in carbohydrate. If the craving for something sweet becomes overwhelming, try a few strawberries, blueberries, or raspberries, and then test your blood sugar one hour later to see if it significantly increases.

Beverages

These high-carbohydrate beverages should be avoided while on a ketogenic diet:

- Non-diet sodas that often contain large amounts of high-fructose corn syrup
- Sweet alcohol sources such as liquors, sweet drinks, and dessert wines
- Malt beverages and beers
- Juices made from fruits and vegetables that are very high in sugar (several tablespoons of lemon or lime juice are okay)
- Milk (whole, skim, and 2%)
- Sweetened varieties of almond and coconut milk

Tips on Avoiding High-Carb Favorites

Here are some tips on using substitutions to ease cravings for restricted high-carb foods.

> If you really like to have a sweet-tasting soda, try the Zevia brand. It's made with stevia. You can also try the Hansen's diet brand which uses Splenda.

> Try flavored sparkling water for a fizzy drink. You can add liquid stevia or sucralose for a "soda" experience.

> Put 1 to 2 tablespoons of heavy cream in a cold glass, and slowly pour in a cold Zevia root-beer drink for a "root-beer float."

> Try adding low-carb syrups to flavor drinks and foods. Da Vinci and Monin brands have sugar-free syrups in some great flavors that are excellent when added to a mixture of softened cream cheese, whipped cream, and sour cream to make a dessert. Make sure to order the sugar-free kind as they have the same flavors in their sugar-sweetened form.

> Make "chocolate candy" by melting coconut oil with unsweetened chocolate and ground nuts. Add sucralose and erythritol sweeteners (Truvia) to taste.

> If you love bread and crackers, you can bake tasty low-carb substitutes from almond or coconut flour. See the Ketogenic Diet Resource website for some great recipes. Googling low-carb bread will provide even more choices.

> Good low-carb mashed potatoes and tasty corn grits can be made by substituting cauliflower in place of the potatoes and corn. Googling should reveal a recipe or two.

> White turnips make an excellent potato substitute for making hash browns. Simply shred and fry in butter. They are great cut into chunks for a beef stew too.

> Make sugar-free gelatin, and add whipped heavy cream to it.

5

Personalizing a Ketogenic Diet

Following a ketogenic diet involves knowing what to eat and how much to eat within the parameters of the diet. The goal of a ketogenic diet plan is to determine how many calories you need to maintain or achieve your ideal body weight, and then figure out the right amount of fat, protein and carbohydrate to eat within that calorie limit. This result should help you get to or maintain your ideal weight while also achieving nutritional ketosis.

In this chapter, we present a step-by-step method we've developed to help your build your own customized ketogenic diet. To begin, let's discuss the three easy rules to follow when implementing the diet.

Start a Ketogenic Diet with Three Rules

Rule 1:

Limit protein intake to what is needed for "repair and maintenance." For most people this will range from 1 to 1.5 grams of protein/kg of goal body weight. Appendix B provides recommended ranges of protein intake based on goal body weight.

Rule 2:

Restrict carbohydrate intake to below 50 grams per day to remain in ketosis, or if you choose not to enjoy the advantages of ketosis, then restrict carbohydrates as much as is tolerable for you. Remember, the more carbohydrates a diabetic consumes, the greater the likelihood of both hyperglycemia and hypoglycemia. This is exactly what we would like to avoid. The carbohydrates you do choose to include in your ketogenic diet should contain lots of nutrients and be lower in energy density. Examples include non-starchy vegetables, nuts, seeds, and low-sugar fruits like berries and avocados. Having small amounts of refined carbohydrate junk foods, even if your total falls below 50 grams per day, will not benefit you.

Rule 3:

Dietary fat intake depends on your weight goals and activity level. Generally, you want to eat enough fat to feel satisfied and maintain a normal weight. If you have excess body fat to shed, you may need to limit dietary fat intake and calories so that you burn stored body fat instead. Step 4 in the next section will give the details.

Five Steps to Personalize Ketogenic Meals

Below is an overview of the steps that will guide you in implementing a ketogenic diet personalized for your goals and needs.

Step 1: Choose your goal body weight and determine the calories needed to maintain it

Step 2: Find your daily protein intake range

Step 3: Determine your carbohydrate tolerance level

Step 4: Calculate your fat allowance

Step 5: Use your macronutrient amounts to choose foods in the correct proportions

Now that we have an overview of the process, let's walk through each of the five steps using a hypothetical example for our friend Sue Dieter.

Sue Dieter is a thirty-two-year-old female who is five foot six and weighs 150 pounds. Her job is sedentary, but she walks one mile three times a week. She would like to use a ketogenic diet to control her blood sugars and avoid diabetic complications, and she would also like to take off ten pounds.

Step 1: Choose your goal body weight and determine the calories needed to maintain it

Choose your goal weight based on the weight at which you feel best. This may be your current weight or a weight you want to reach. After you decide on a goal weight, use an online calorie calculator (for example, the CI Medical Center has one on their website under "Health Tools"[49]) or use your own experience to determine a daily calorie target. Use your goal body weight in the calculator to factor in your activity levels.

Sue decides that she feels best at 140 pounds, so she sets that as her goal body weight. She then uses a calorie calculator to figure out a general daily calorie target, and she factors in her activity level to achieve her weight loss goal. Sue looks at the data she gets from the calculator and decides on the calorie goal she will set:

- Height: 5'6"
- Goal Body Weight: 140
- Daily Calorie Needs: 1500

Step 2: Find your daily protein-intake range

As we discussed earlier (Basic Rules for Implementing a Ketogenic Diet), protein intake on a ketogenic diet should range from 1 to 1.5 grams/kg goal body weight per day. The lower end of the range will facilitate weight loss, if needed. However, do not reduce protein intake below 1 gram per kg of goal body weight per day.

If you are consuming 1 gram/kg of goal body weight per day and are still not shedding body fat, then reduce the amount of fat you are eating (which will be discussed in Step 4). In addition, don't go above the top end of your protein range because excess amounts of protein may increase blood sugar. Although there is a table of daily protein recommendations in appendix B, here's how Sue would determine the grams of protein she needs each day.

> Sue set her goal body weight in Step 1 at 140 pounds. She divides 140 pounds by 2.2 to arrive at her goal body weight in kilograms; this equals 63.6 kilograms, which she rounds to 64 kg. At one gram per kilogram of ideal body weight, the now knows her minimum protein intake is 64 grams. She multiplies 64 by 1.5 to get 96, the top end of her protein range. This puts her range at 64 to 96 grams of protein/day.

Step 3: Determine your carbohydrate tolerance level

Your carbohydrate tolerance level can range from 20 to 50 grams per day, with the low end better suited for weight loss. As mentioned, most diabetics would do well to limit carbohydrate intake to below 50 total grams per day to remain in ketosis. If you choose to avoid nutritional ketosis, restrict carbohydrates as much as is tolerable for you.

Although recommendations are to keep carbohydrate intake below 50 grams per day, you can start at 50 to 100 grams per day to allow time to adapt to both the diet and lower blood sugar and insulin. This slower introduction may minimize the likelihood of hypoglycemia and help you adjust your blood-sugar medications. To start slowly, try 5- to 10-gram reductions of daily carb intake on a weekly basis until you reach a low of 20 to 50 carb grams per day. For instance, you might start week one at 100 grams per day. Then during week two, reduce intake to 90 grams per day, and during week three, reduce to 80 grams per day and so on.

> Sue decides to start at 30 total grams of carbs per day. She plans to monitor how she feels and check her blood-glucose response at each meal to assess whether her carb limits are appropriate.

Total Carbs versus Net Carbs

A question we are asked frequently is whether to count total carbohydrates or "net" carbs. In general, many carb counting resources advise that net carbs (grams) = total carbs (grams) minus dietary fiber (grams) minus sugar alcohols (grams).

Dietary fiber is utilized by your gut bacteria to make short-chain fatty acids (acetate, propionate, and butyrate) which are then primarily utilized by your colon cells for energy. Thus, dietary fiber does not raise blood glucose in those with diabetes. In fact, a study published in the *New England Journal of Medicine* showed that subjects with type 2 diabetes experienced a reduction in blood glucose when they consumed 50 grams of dietary fiber per day.[50] In contrast, sugar alcohols (e.g. maltitol, erythritol, glycerol, hydrogenated starch hydrolysates, xylitol) do have absorbable calories and do raise blood glucose and thus should *not* be included in the formula for net carbs.

Hence, we think net carbohydrate should be calculated as follows: *Net carbs (grams) = (grams of total carbs) - (grams of dietary fiber)*. In other words, subtract grams of fiber, but not sugar alcohol carbs, from total carbs when counting.

Step 4: Calculate your fat allowance

Your fat intake is determined by subtracting your protein and carb calories from your total calorie target. Protein and carbohydrates have 4 calories per gram and fat has 9 calories per gram.

Sue uses the top end of her protein gram range to perform the following simple calculations. Her choice is arbitrary, as she knows she can always reduce protein intake should that become necessary.

Since protein and carbohydrates both have the same number of calories per gram (4), Sue adds them together. She adds 96 (grams of protein) plus 30 (grams of carbohydrate), which equals 126 grams, and then multiplies that number by 4 calories: 126 grams times 4 equals 504 calories. So Sue can have about 500 calories of protein and carbohydrate (combined) each day).

Next, Sue subtracts that amount from her daily calorie target of 1500 calories: 1500 minus 504 equals 996 calories.

Sue now knows she can have about 1000 calories of fat each day. She divides 1000 by 9 to figure out how many grams of fat that would be, which works out to about 111 grams of fat each day.

The amount of fat you can eat to maintain ideal weight depends loosely on your energy expenditure and weight status. You need enough fat to get your essential fatty acids and absorb fat-soluble vitamins. Sufficient fat in your diet also helps prevent your metabolism from behaving like it's starving (i.e., slowing down).

Eating an equal or greater amount of fat than you need means your body will use what you eat first, and body fat will either remain the same or increase. Following a ketogenic diet can facilitate fat loss, but it does not guarantee it. A good place to start for reducing fat intake is to cut back on high-fat calorie foods such as nuts, cream, and cheese. If you are not reaching your weight-loss goals, try reducing your daily fat intake by 10 grams (say from 100 to 90 grams) and maintaining this new number for one week. After one week, if needed, reduce the daily fat intake another 10 grams. Continue this weekly reduction process until weight loss begins and then stay at that level.

Correct adjustment of all three dietary macronutrients (carbohydrate, protein, and fat) is necessary for reducing body-fat stores. If you have excess weight to lose, and these steps don't resolve the issue, we recommend you consult with a physician or nutritionist who is knowledgeable in ketogenic diets. A solution is available, but sometimes it takes an expert to sort out the source of the problem. There could be undiagnosed medical problems or medications that need to be addressed that are preventing body-fat loss.

Step 5: Use your macronutrient amounts to choose foods in the correct proportions

Once you have figured out your macronutrient amounts, you can decide how to divide them over the day. We recommend the use of free websites such as myfitnesspal.com or cronometer.com to track your intake and take the aggravation out of staying on target.

Sue now knows she can have the following amounts of macronutrients on a daily basis:

- 64 to 96 grams of protein
- 30 grams of carbohydrate
- 111 grams of fat

Sue divides her target macronutrient amounts and calorie intake by the number of meals she eats. For instance, if she eats three meals each day, her targets might look like this:

Total Daily Calories: 1500 calories divided over three meals each day is about 500 calories per meal

Protein: 64 to 96 grams divided over three meals each day is 21-32 grams of protein at each meal

Carbs: 30 grams divided over three meals each day is 10 grams of carbohydrate per meal

Fat: 111 grams divided over three meals each day is 37 grams of fat at each meal

Using the Food Lists

Food choices are usually a combination of fat, protein, and carb. We've built some food lists in appendix C that include the amount of each macronutrient for common types of foods. You can also use any food-count book that includes all the macronutrients, or you can use an online food-tracking website such as www.myfitnesspal.com or www.cronometer.com.

> If Sue doesn't mind tracking her food intake on paper, she can now go to the food lists in appendix C and pick out the foods she wants to eat that match her daily macronutrient amounts. She can also use a food-counter book or an online food-tracking database to choose her foods.

Making It Easy

Using a tracking website such as myfitnesspal.com or cronometer.com makes it easy to select the right amount of foods that fit within your mealtime macronutrient allowances. We highly recommend using this approach as you can readily adjust amounts of each food until you have the right balance of macronutrients. Regardless of how you determine what to eat for each of your meals, it's important that you write down or print out the meals you plan to prepare on a regular basis. This eliminates the need to repeatedly look up or calculate amounts. For every recipe you have at your fingertips, implementing the diet will become that much easier.

A Few Example Meals for a 150-Pound Person

These meals are designed for a 150-pound person and are in perfect ketogenic ratios. Adjust the amounts for your physical measurements and your custom macronutrient needs.

Eggs and Bacon with Spinach

In 24 grams of butter, sauté about 15 grams of white onion, and cook until soft. Throw in 1 cup of raw spinach, and cook until wilted. Make 2 wells in the onion and spinach mixture, and add a large egg in each well. Cook until eggs are done. Top off with 3 or 4 slices of cooked bacon.

Beef and Onion with Egg

Sauté 30 grams of onion in 24 grams of butter until the onion is soft. Add 100 grams of 80/20 ground beef, and cook until beef is browned. Add rosemary and thyme to flavor. Finally, add two egg yolks and cook to desired yolk doneness.

Smoked Salmon and Cream Cheese

Combine 120 grams of smoked salmon with 30 grams of cream cheese and 25 grams of white onion. Add dill or other spices to your liking. Wrap spoonfuls of the mixture in green lettuce leaves to make a salmon roll.

Baked Chicken Thigh with Green Salad

Slice a baked chicken thigh (weighing 150 grams before it was cooked) off the bone with the skin. Serve over a salad of 100 grams of lettuce, 10 grams of sliced onion, and 10 grams of radish; dress with 15 grams of olive oil and 10 grams of red wine vinegar.

Pork Ribs with Cabbage

Sauté 127 grams of country-style pork rib meat cut into small chunks in 27 grams of butter until almost cooked. Add 85 grams of shredded cabbage, and cook until done.

Chicken Breast with Onions and Hummus

Sauté 130 grams of sliced, boneless chicken breast and 30 grams of onion in 27 grams of butter until almost cooked. Add 24 grams of classic hummus, and stir to make a nice sauce over the chicken.

Baked Salmon and Broccoli

Lay a 140-gram salmon fillet in a piece of foil, and add 38 grams of butter. Seal foil around salmon and butter, and bake at 350 degrees for about 20 minutes. When the fish flakes in thickest part, it's done. While the salmon bakes, steam 75 grams of broccoli in a double boiler. Serve the broccoli with the baked salmon, ladling melted butter over all.

Tips on Using Your Customized Diet Plan

> Try not to eat all of your macronutrients at one meal. Eating large amounts of food in one sitting will spike blood sugar and insulin. The goal for blood sugar and insulin is low and steady, so it's important to divide up your total macronutrient intake over several meals throughout the day.

> Americans are used to using ounce measurements, but if you prefer to use gram weights when weighing foods, either will work. We've provided a conversion table in appendix D.

> If you like to have smaller and more frequent meals, you may need to divide your carbohydrates up between only a couple of meals, having no carbohydrates during the other meals. Otherwise, it becomes challenging to stick to such small carbohydrate allowances at each meal.

> Think outside the box. Eggs and bacon can be eaten at lunch or dinner, and steak with vegetables makes a great breakfast.

> If the foods you like aren't included in the Food Lists section, you can use an online food-tracking program or a food reference book that provides carb, protein, and fat gram counts for foods.

> Mix and match food choices as you wish, as long as you stay within the macronutrient levels for your ideal weight.

> Pay attention to tracking your choices correctly. Some food choices will count as a protein and fat; some will count as a combination of protein, fat, and carbohydrate. Remember, carbohydrates have to be counted, whether they are consumed as part of a fat or protein food or consumed as a food from the carbohydrate list.

> It will probably be easier if you start with using "food units" instead of preparing complex meals that require measuring multiple ingredients. Examples of food units are listed here: eggs, avocados, sausage links, bacon strips, pats of butter, cubes of cheese, shrimp, and hamburger patties.

> Choosing fattier protein sources, such as 80/20 ground beef and salmon, over lean meats, such as chicken breast and shrimp, will make it easier to stay within your protein gram range.

> Buy meat in bulk packages, and divide it into smaller portions. For instance, say you can have 135 grams of meat in your meals. Buy 80/20 ground beef in five-pound packages. At home, break it into 135 gram portions, shape each one into a patty, wrap it in plastic wrap, and place the patties in a freezer bag for storage. When you want beef, take one patty out of the freezer, and you're ready to go.

6

Cooking, Dining Out and Traveling

One of the keys to the successful implementation of a ketogenic diet is choosing and eating fresh food. Cooking skills and making the right choices when dining out and traveling are important, so in this chapter, we will discuss how to prepare and choose the right foods while on a ketogenic diet.

Ketogenic Cooking Techniques

Ketogenic cooking is all about creating meals from fresh, basic ingredients. Each meal should be based on a protein source such as beef, pork, poultry, or seafood, which is cooked or dressed with natural fats such as butter, olive oil, or coconut oil. Low-carbohydrate vegetables and salads with dressings complement the meal. Sauces and dressings are all made of natural fats and added as you like. Sauces and dressings are the key to taking a ketogenic meal from okay to fabulous.

The main challenge in preparing ketogenic meals is to substitute new keto-friendly cooking techniques for traditional cooking methods. For instance, stew and chili recipes usually start with coating the meat in flour. For a ketogenic stew, the flour is eliminated. To thicken stew near the end of the cooking process, some of the cooked vegetables can be pureed with a portion of the liquid and then returned to the pot to make a thicker final product. Another way to thicken stews and sauces is to cook them longer to reduce the water and thicken the remaining liquid.

Beef, pork, poultry, and seafood choices should be prepared using the following methods: roasting, grilling, poaching, baking, sautéing, broiling, and steaming. No flour, breading, or cracker crumbs should be used, as they add carbohydrates. The same goes for cooking vegetables. All of the methods mentioned above are good. Be aware that cooking vegetables in water (wet-heat cooking) can destroy the vitamins, so steaming is better. If you are making a stew, at least some of vitamins are recovered because the cooking water becomes part of the final meal.

Useful Kitchen Supplies

A nonstick skillet, a food scale, a high-heat spatula, and parchment paper can be used daily while on a ketogenic diet. You will find that these and other supplies are indispensable for making your life easier:

- Heat-resistant silicone spatulas for scraping all fat from cookware (small ones work great for scooping up salad dressing from the bottom of a bowl)
- Digital food scale with ounce and gram measurements
- Travel cooler and freezer packs for bringing food to work or along on leisure activities
- Small plastic containers with snap-on lids with silicone seals
- Small wire whisks to incorporate oils into a sauce or dressing
- Handheld immersion blender
- Parchment paper for baking
- Nonstick frying pans
- Silicone muffin pans and cookie-sheet liners
- Food processor
- Glass measuring cups in 2-, 4- and 8-cup sizes
- Ceramic quiche pan or deep-dish pie plate
- Single-serving glass bowls with plastic lids

- Krups Egg Cooker (nutritionist Amy Berger of Tuit Nutrition says this is the best thirty dollars you'll ever spend.)

Time-Saving Cooking Tips

If time is short during the week, the following list offers some ways to stay on track.

> Cook all your food for the coming week on the weekend. For example, you can roast a chicken, debone it, and make part of it into chicken salad. Or bake a beef or pork shoulder, and slice it for easy snacks.

> Make egg salad, tuna salad, and other meat salads; these are easy and fast.

> Prepare vegetable casseroles ahead of time for a quick side-dish option.

> Cook stews or beef chili in a slow cooker or electric pressure cooker (such as an Instant Pot) and freeze them in single-serving containers.

> Make homemade hollandaise sauce, pesto, and other fat-based sauces and dressings, and store them in the refrigerator so you can grab a quick spoonful to add to cooked meat

> Stock the cupboard and refrigerator with easy-to-fix, low-carbo-hydrate foods: canned tuna and chicken, sardines, or hard-boiled eggs for egg salad. A mixture of mayonnaise and cream cheese makes a great dressing for tuna or chicken salad. Mayonnaise and melted butter mixed together tastes great on egg salad or when spread on hard-boiled eggs.

> If you cook in the evening, make extra servings, and store them for the next meal.

> Learn new, more efficient ways to cook. For instance, lay out bacon on a cookie sheet and bake it in the oven. It's easier and less messy than frying it in a skillet.

> Find local sources with low-carbohydrate food offerings. A local deli may have chicken salads, baked fish, and other low-carbohydrate choices. Or, look for specialty restaurants that have meat kabobs or chef salads that you can buy on the run.

What if I Hate to Cook?

Grocery stores, Sam's Club, Costco, and other big-box stores offer cooked meats, roasted chickens, boiled eggs, ready-to-eat bacon, packaged deli meats, cheeses, and fresh vegetables. Most grocery-store seafood departments will steam shrimp for you. Canned tuna, chicken, and salmon mixed with mayonnaise and cream cheese and served over cucumbers with avocado makes a good lunch choice. Salads with full-fat dressing, avocado, and chopped prepared meats are also a great option.

In addition, you may have a local Whole Foods with a smoked-meat department or a delicatessen that offers a variety of cooked foods. Plain Greek yogurt mixed with your choice of spices and sweetener is very satisfying as a dessert.

Quick Ketogenic Snack Ideas

If you are in a pinch for a quick bite to eat, here are some suggestions to get you started.

- Spread a slice of ham, turkey, or salami with cream cheese or mayonnaise, add a slice of cheese, and roll it up by itself or in a lettuce leaf
- Wrap cooked bacon, tomato chunks, and mayonnaise or cream cheese in a lettuce leaf
- Cut cooked steak, pork, or chicken into small pieces and mix with mayonnaise, sour cream, cream cheese, or avocado
- Deviled eggs, or hard-boiled eggs sliced and spread with mayonnaise or sour cream
- Baked chicken wings (no breading) and blue-cheese dip

- Smoked-salmon slices spread with cream cheese mixed with dill and lemon juice
- Smoked salmon mixed with scrambled eggs and topped with cream cheese
- Crab meat mixed with cream cheese and lemon juice on cucumber slices
- Shrimp with minced onion, mayonnaise, and dried dill on cucumber slices
- Beef jerky cured without sugar
- Antipasto made from peppers, olives, prosciutto or salami, and cheese cubes
- Tuna mixed with mayonnaise and cream cheese and piled on cucumber rounds
- Roasted or raw nuts
- Olives stuffed with feta cheese
- Dill pickles with cheddar cheese
- Pork rinds dipped in a mixture of full-fat sour cream and low-carbohydrate salsa
- Pork rinds dipped in ranch dressing or pesto sauce
- Jicama, radishes, or turnip sticks with full-fat sour-cream dip or ranch dressing
- Celery stuffed with a cream cheese/blue-cheese mixture
- Celery stuffed with cream cheese mixed with curry or any other spice you like
- Celery stuffed with almond butter
- Macadamia nuts fried in butter and sprinkled with cinnamon
- Pecans with thin slices of blue cheese
- Chunks of avocado and tomatoes mixed with mayonnaise
- Steamed or boiled shrimp with dill mayonnaise
- String cheese and pepperoni slices
- Cucumber and tomato chunks with feta cheese and balsamic vinegar

- Sliced radishes spread with cream cheese and sprinkled with chives or spices
- Shrimp mixed with a low-carb Thai green-chili sauce and sprinkled with cilantro
- Mix crispy cooked bacon and blue cheese with sour cream, then add spices to taste (this makes a good dip for raw broccoli and cauliflower or leftover cooked chicken)
- Mix ¼ cup of almond butter and a little heavy cream and sweetener of your choice
- Mix 2 ounces of cream cheese with 2 tablespoons heavy cream and sweetener
- Greek yogurt mixed with cardamom, ginger, cinnamon, and sweetener
- Low-carb, sugar-free popsicles
- Mix 2 ounces of goat cheese with a 1/4 cup of blueberries and stevia

Recipe Resources

The following recipe sites are useful as a guide. Typing "low-carbohydrate recipes" into Google will provide more sites with recipes to peruse as well.

- www.ketogenic-diet-resource.com/low-carb-recipes.html
- www.charliefoundation.org/
- www.atkins.com/recipes.aspx
- www.alldayidreamaboutfood.com/
- www.genaw.com/lowcarb/
- www.healthyindulgences.net/
- www.amongfriends.us/
- www.uplateanyway.com/keto/
- www.comfybelly.com/2012/06/baking-with-coconut-flour-2/ (for a page on baking with coconut flour)
- www.comfybelly.com/2009/01/baking-with-almond-flour/ (for a page on cooking with almond flour)

- www.breatheimhungry.com
- www.authoritynutrition.com/101-healthy-low-carb-recipes/
- www.yourlighterside.com

Low-Carbohydrate Cookbooks

These books provide more ideas for meal planning and include techniques for preparing foods. Not all of the recipes are specifically ketogenic, but they should help in generating ideas for variety in your meals.

- *500 Low-Carb Recipes* by Dana Carpender. This goes in and out of print.
- *200 Low-Carb, High-Fat Recipes: Easy Recipes to Jumpstart Your Low-Carb Weight Loss* by Dana Carpender
- *300 15-Minute Low-Carb Recipes* by Dana Carpender
- *Eating Stella Style* by George Stella
- *George Stella's Livin' Low Carb* by George Stella and Cory Williamson
- *The Ketogenic Kitchen* by Patricia Daly and Dominic Kemp *New Atkins for a New You Cookbook* by Colette Heimowitz
- *Fat Fast Cookbook* by Dana Carpender
- *Paleo Cooking* by Elana Amsterdam
- *Low Carbing Among Friends (all volumes)* by Jennifer Eloff
- *Nourished: A Cookbook for Health, Weight Loss, and Metabolic Balance* by Judy Barnes Baker, Jacqueline Eberstein, RN, and Richard Feinman, PhD
- *Carb Wars: Sugar is the New Fat* by Judy Barnes Baker
- *The Low-Carb Comfort Food Cookbook Paperback* by Ursula Solom, Mary Dan Eades, and Michael R Eades
- *Extreme Lo-Carb Cuisine: 250 Recipes With Virtually No Carbohydrates* by Sharron Long
- *Low-Carb Gourmet* by Karen Barnaby
- *Muffins to Slim By: Fast Low-Carb, Gluten-Free Bread & Muffin Recipes to Mix and Microwave in a Mug (Volume 1)* by Em Elless

- *The Low Carb High Fat Cookbook: 100 Recipes to Lose Weight and Feel Great* by Sten Sture Skaldeman
- *Fat: An Appreciation of a Misunderstood Ingredient, with Recipes* by Jennifer McLagan
- *The Keto Cookbook* by Dawn Martenz. There is a Kindle and paperback version. The paperback version is better, as the Kindle version is not formatted in a way that is easy to use.

In addition, most whole-food recipes from your favorite cookbook can be adapted to a low-carb, ketogenic version.

Dining Out on a Ketogenic Diet

Many people want to know if they can eat at restaurants while on a ketogenic diet. The short answer is yes! You can enjoy dining out while on a ketogenic diet, provided you're careful about what you order. Being on this diet should not prevent you from enjoying a nice meal with friends and family. Don't be shy about customizing your order and asking for substitutions when necessary. As people become more health conscious and food allergies become more common, waitstaff are not put off by special requests. Here is a guide to selecting appropriate foods that will allow you to continue getting the benefits of your unique diet.

General Tips

Your best bet for staying on plan is to choose simply prepared dishes. Choose meats, poultry, and seafood which have been grilled, baked, or roasted. Non-starchy vegetables or salads are good side choices, but if any meat, chicken or shrimp is served on the salad, make sure it hasn't been breaded. Low fat salad dressings usually contain sugar, so select either full fat kinds or oil and vinegar. In addition, avoid all pasta, rice, bread, potatoes, corn, beans, soda, and desserts (including fruit). You should also avoid sauces and soups . They are usually thickened with sugar, flour, or cornstarch.

Another strategy is to prepare before you go. Most restaurants have their menus posted online. Look in advance to see what will be suitable for you so you'll have an easier time ordering. If you're dining with friends and the restaurant of choice isn't conducive to a low-carb meal, simply suggest a change of location.

Tips for Specific Cuisines

> *Mexican*: Fajitas are a great choice; decline the chips and tortillas, and ask for extra vegetables instead of beans and/or rice. Fajita fillings are just grilled meat and vegetables, and you can enjoy sour cream and small amounts of cheese, guacamole, and pico de gallo as condiments. Be sure there's no corn in the pico de gallo. (At Chipotle and Qdoba, you can get meat, lettuce, and vegetables in a bowl rather than in a tortilla.)

> *Chinese/Japanese:* Ask for your dishes to be prepared steamed or with no sauce. (Sauces typically contain sugar and corn starch.) Use soy sauce or hot mustard as condiments. Great choices for Chinese takeout are steamed chicken or shrimp with mixed vegetables. Some restaurants also offer grilled chicken/beef on skewers. Avoid rice, noodles, wontons, dumplings, deep-fried foods, and tempura (due to the breading). Sashimi and sushi are tasty; just avoid the rice.

> *Italian:* Pasta is obviously not permitted, but most Italian restaurants have many other options that are suitable for a very low-carbohydrate diet. Choose salads, steaks, chicken, pork, or seafood with vegetables. Avoid bread and breadsticks, and ask for no croutons on your salad. Ask for extra non-starchy green leafy vegetables as side dishes instead of pasta or potatoes. Antipasto (an olive, meat, and cheese platter) is also a good option.

> *Chain restaurants:* You can find suitable choices at chain restaurants like Applebee's, Chili's, Olive Garden, and Outback Steakhouse. Just ask for the appropriate substitutions. For example, ask for double

broccoli instead of a potato, and avoid the bread they bring as an appetizer.

› *Middle Eastern/Greek:* Choose kebabs or other grilled-meat dishes. Ask for extra vegetables or meat instead of rice or pita bread. Avoid hummus, stuffed grape leaves (they usually contain rice), anything else with beans, and high-starch foods such as potatoes.

› *Diner/American bistro:* These restaurants usually have a very diverse menu, and finding suitable options will be easy. Just use the same logic as for anywhere else: no grain or other starchy carbohydrates and no sweets for dessert. Fantastic choices are Cobb, chef, or Caesar salads (no croutons) with full-fat dressing. Perfectly fine choices are hamburgers or sandwiches without the bun or bread. Always ask for non-starchy vegetables (like greens) instead of fries or other potato sides. You can often substitute a simple house salad for a starchy side dish. Other good selections include any type of roasted meat, chicken, or fish or a platter of egg or tuna salad on a bed of lettuce.

› *Breakfast:* Stick with eggs, bacon, ham, and sausage. Avoid pancakes, waffles, potatoes, toast, bagels, muffins, fruit, juice, and jam or jelly. Western omelets are a great option (eggs, ham, onion, peppers), as are any type of omelet that contains eggs, meat, cheese, and/or low-starch veggies (peppers, spinach, mushrooms, onions, zucchini). Any other eggs are great, too: poached, scrambled, over easy, or hard-boiled. Avoid bottled ketchup that contains high-fructose corn syrup. Use mustard, mayonnaise, or hot sauce as condiments.

› *Salads:* Customize your salad as necessary: no dried cranberries, fruit, croutons, or crunchy noodles. Stick with lettuce, spinach, and other greens. Suitable additions are chopped hard-boiled egg, bacon, cheese, avocado, ham, turkey, chicken, steak, salmon, olives, cucumbers, sliced peppers, radishes, and other non-starchy vegetables. Use oil and vinegar or a high-fat dressing like ranch or blue cheese. Avoid thousand island, French, honey mustard, raspberry vinaigrette, and other sweetened dressings. (Besides olive oil, you can use avocado or macadamia oil to make delicious homemade vinaigrettes.)

Beware of Hidden Dining Pitfalls

Restaurant staff use many different techniques to prepare and present food. Sugar is often added to enhance flavors. Don't be shy about asking your server for details on how foods are prepared. For instance, some restaurants add flour or pancake batter to their eggs to make omelets fluffier. Ask if this is the case, and, if so, ask if they'll prepare your eggs without that. (Another way around this is to stick with hard-boiled, poached, over easy or sunny-side up.)

If there is a sauce with ingredients you're not sure of, ask the server to tell you what's in it. Many sauces contain sugar, corn syrup, corn starch, and/or flour. It's best to stay with simply prepared dishes to avoid this. Also, be careful with condiments. Ketchup is generally loaded with high-fructose corn syrup, and many salad dressings are high in sugar and corn syrup. Your best bets for condiments (if you need them at all) are the ones listed here:

- Mustard (any kind except honey mustard)
- Mayonnaise
- Hot sauce
- Melted butter
- Olive oil
- Macadamia oil
- Vinegar (red wine, apple cider, white)

Full-fat, low-carbohydrate salad dressings are also permitted. Look at labels in supermarkets to determine which types are best. The carbohydrate count in a 2-tablespoon serving should be 2 grams or less.

Travel Tips

With thanks to Miriam Kalamian of dietarytherapies.com, the tips below will help you stay on track if you have to travel. We've tried to cover various travel situations, including how to avoid the high-carb options offered at conferences.

Automobile

- Pack a cooler with small plastic containers of your favorite meals. You are less likely to stray from your plan if you have familiar foods at hand.
- Carry small packages of nuts and individually wrapped cheese sticks. This is also a good idea if going by airplane.
- Bring water, and stay well hydrated!

Air Travel

- TSA may allow food and liquids for consumption during your flight if you notify them that you have diabetes. Call first to be sure; rules change over time.
- Choose salads with protein (chicken, boiled egg, deli ham, sliced cheese) at the airport. Choose salad dressings with the least amount of carbohydrate per serving. Look for mayonnaise packets to use with the protein. You can also eat chilled butter pats.
- Pack protein powder in sealable plastic sandwich bags and bring a plastic shake-maker bottle. In a pinch, you can make a shake with water.
- If you're checking a bag, you can bring your favorite (unopened) salad dressing and a jar of olives. Triple bag this in plastic and add a note explaining what it is (TSA may want to know). Bring clean plastic bags to store leftovers for the return trip.
- It's a good idea to have a supply of glucose tablets or gels in your carry-on bag just in case.

Conferences

Standard meals offered at conferences are a mine field! Ask about food options when you register.

- If you are attending a conference which spans several days, visit the closest local grocery store once you arrive and buy some non-perishable foods such as jerky or nuts, or bring them from home. If you have access to a refrigerator in your hotel room, buy lunch meat and cheese slices to have on hand.
- Breakfast: Stick to scrambled or boiled eggs with bacon, sausage, or cheese. Eat chilled butter pats for extra fat. Ask for half-and-half or heavy cream instead of milk or creamer.
- Lunch: Choose deli meats, tuna, or chicken salad. Scrap the bread and double the salad veggies (minus carrots). Look for olive oil and vinegar (avoid balsamic).
- Dinner: Choose simple, whole meats, grilled veggies, no sauces, no breading. Add olive oil and/or butter. Make sure you get all the oils from the bottom of the plate or bowl.
- Snack: Macadamia nuts are perfect! You may also want to take along individually wrapped cheddar cheese pieces.

Social Events

- Bring your own meal or eat before you arrive. It's difficult to fight off the "Please, just have one bite" or "But I made this just for you" comments if you're hungry or don't have an alternative.

Part 3

Managing Blood Sugar and Insulin

7

Type 1 Diabetes Mellitus

T1DM is an autoimmune disease affecting children and adolescents in which the affected person's immune system mistakenly attacks pancreatic beta cells. This results in a loss of ability to produce insulin due to beta-cell destruction.

The first manifestation is glucose intolerance, which develops after about 50% of the beta cells have been destroyed. Symptoms of diabetes develop after destruction of 80% to 85% of the beta cells. Fasting blood sugar begins to rise as beta-cell destruction worsens, but if the blood-sugar elevation is mild, there may not be any symptoms. Once hyperglycemia becomes persistent, especially when blood glucose exceeds an average of 180 mg/dL (10.0 mmol/L), the kidney's ability to reabsorb the filltered glucose is exceeded, and glucose is excreted in the urine. This causes two problems.

First, a lack of insulin results in an inability to store fat, an inability to maintain lean muscle tissue[51], and an impaired ability to transport glucose into cells. Energy in the form of glucose is excreted unused in the urine, and large amounts of fatty acids from adipose tissue flow into the blood stream. These excess fatty acids are converted to ketones and some are excreted via the kidneys and breath. The combination of fat-storage dysfunction along with the loss of glucose results in a wasting of muscle and fat tissue and results in significant weight loss.

Second, the presence of glucose in the urine causes more urine volume to be excreted (osmotic diuresis) and acts like a potent diuretic. This causes excessive urination (polyuria) that, in turn, stimulates thirst with an increase in fluid intake (polydipsia). It is not uncommon for people with undiagnosed diabetes to have cravings for sweet foods like ice cream, candy, and sweet drinks like fruit juice, cola, or tea. Because insulin is absent, blood glucose can't be moved into cells for utilization, and the body and brain sense a lack of available glucose despite excess quantities in the bloodstream. The impaired ability to utilize fuels (glucose, fat, and protein) causes fatigue and hunger. Thus, individuals with T1DM usually present with these five symptoms: weight loss, fatigue, hunger, polyuria, and polydipsia. Many other signs and symptoms can occur depending on how long the blood glucose has been elevated. These symptoms include blurred vision, numbness of skin, erectile dysfunction, and unexplained infections.

Approximately 5% to 10% of diabetics are diagnosed with this form of diabetes. Currently, people with type 1 diabetes require daily insulin injections, which they must carefully balance with food intake and exercise-related energy expenditure.

Latent Autoimmune Diabetes in Adults

Latent autoimmune diabetes in adults[52] (LADA) is a variant of T1DM that occurs later in life—from young adults to the elderly—as opposed to T1DM that afflicts children and adolescents. In LADA, beta-cell destruction often occurs slowly, which may explain, in part, why it occurs in older individuals. Occasionally, patients with LADA are misdiagnosed as having T2DM primarily based on their age. Patients with LADA usually are of normal weight or only mildly overweight when they began to lose weight. Weight eventually falls below normal, often before other symptoms of fatigue, increased urination and thirst, or blurred vision begin.

LADA and T1DM are due to insulin deficiency whereas T2DM, at least initially, is due to insulin resistance with compensatory or coexisting hyperinsulinemia. Additionally, individuals with T2DM are usually overweight or obese, and they do not lose weight before the onset of typical symptoms of diabetes. Although there are no definitive lab tests to distinguish LADA from T2DM in adults, the two conditions can be identified by several findings. The following are features of LADA not seen in T2DM:

- Blood glucose meets the criteria for diabetes with loss of weight in a person who was of normal weight or only mildly overweight.
- Fasting insulin level is either below normal or at the lower end of the normal range in the presence of hyperglycemia.
- Oral hypoglycemic medications fail to achieve good blood-glucose control, relief of symptoms, or a return to normal weight, whereas the administration of insulin does.

Some LADA patients may be able to attain optimal blood-glucose control without insulin early in the course of the disease, especially if a ketogenic diet is adopted. This is referred to as the "honeymoon" period. Eventually, insulin will be necessary to control blood-glucose adequately. Experimental research into ways to modulate the immune system to reduce the anti-beta-cell and anti-insulin antibody formation is ongoing.[53]

ADA Blood-Sugar Recommendations

Blood-sugar levels peak at one hour after a carbohydrate meal in both normal and diabetic individuals. Using carbohydrate restriction can control postprandial (after meal) increases in blood glucose and the resulting need for insulin. It can also reduce average blood sugar, thereby improving HbA1c test results. Ultimately, adopting a ketogenic or carbohydrate-restricted diet can improve all diabetic health markers, including fasting and between-meal blood sugars and HbA1c. The long-term result is a reduction in glycation damage, which reduces the likelihood of future diabetic complications. Hence, we think aiming for a blood-glucose target as close to the nondiabetic range as can be accomplished safely is a goal worth pursuing for long-term, positive health benefits. A ketogenic diet can make this goal easier to achieve.

We find it interesting that the 2017 American Diabetes Association guidelines for glycemic control in adults with diabetes are as follows:

- A reasonable A1C goal for many nonpregnant adults is <7% (53 mmol/mol).

- Providers might reasonably suggest more stringent A1C goals (such as <6.5% [48 mmol/mol]) for selected individual patients if this can be achieved without significant hypoglycemia or other adverse effects of treatment (i.e., polypharmacy). Appropriate patients might include those with short duration of diabetes, type 2 diabetes treated with lifestyle or metformin only, long life expectancy, or no significant cardiovascular disease.

- Less stringent A1C goals (such as <8% [64 mmol/mol]) may be appropriate for patients with a history of severe hypoglycemia, limited life expectancy, advanced microvascular or macrovascular complications, extensive comorbid conditions, or long-standing diabetes in whom the goal is difficult to achieve despite diabetes self-management education, appropriate glucose monitoring, and effective doses of multiple glucose-lowering agents including insulin.[54]

Why doesn't the American Diabetes Association (ADA) advocate normal blood-glucose values? We think it's because trying to achieve that level of blood-glucose control while consuming the ADA-recommended high-carbohydrate diet and taking insulin is not possible without numerous and potentially dangerous hypoglycemic episodes.

Understandably, the ADA does not want to recommend a treatment plan that would cause life-threatening hypoglycemia, but their solution is to advocate elevated blood sugars long-term, and this is precisely what causes the severe and often fatal complications of diabetes.

Although these recommendations are understandable in the context of a diet containing the currently recommended intake of 45 to 60 grams of carbohydrate at each meal, we believe a ketogenic diet could offer diabetics an effective tool for better control of both hyperglycemia and hypoglycemia and provide a significant reduction in the risk of long-term diabetic complications associated with glycation damage.

8

Blood-Sugar Management for T1DM

In this chapter, we'll discuss the skills and tools needed for managing blood sugar and the importance of accurate blood-sugar monitoring and testing in the management of long-term diabetic complications. We'll also present symptoms of and treatment for hypoglycemia and hyperglycemia and discuss the benefits and drawbacks of HbA1c and fructosamine testing.

Why Blood Glucose Is So Variable for Type 1 Diabetics

For people with type 1 diabetes, there are three reasons why blood sugar levels vary despite best efforts for successful control.

Reason 1: Dietary Carbohydrates

We have established the fact that, upon digestion, dietary carbohydrate is converted into glucose and requires more insulin to convert it into glycogen or fat than does dietary protein or fat. Restricting dietary carbohydrate thus ameliorates hyperglycemia and reduces the need for exogenous insulin. (*Exogenous* denotes "from outside the body," and so, exogenous insulin is insulin that is injected or infused.)

In addition, trying to balance dietary carbohydrate with exogenous insulin is very imprecise because of the inaccuracy of published dietary carbohydrate on food labels. It varies by ±50%, as pointed out in a study on low carbohydrate diets for type 1 diabetes by Vesti Nielen et al.[55] Since trying to accurately match dietary carbohydrate with exogenous insulin is virtually impossible, carbohydrate counting is of little to no value. This was shown in a study titled "Efficacy of carbohydrate counting in type 1 diabetes: a systematic review and meta-analysis"[56] and in another study by Laurenzi et al. titled "Effects of Carbohydrate Counting on Glucose Control and Quality of Life Over 24 Weeks in Adult Patients With Type 1 Diabetes on Continuous Subcutaneous Insulin Infusion."[57]

Reason 2: Exogenous Insulin

Injected or pumped exogenous insulin is life-saving, and persons with T1DM should be grateful for its availability, especially the insulin analogs that more closely approximate normal insulin secretion. Nevertheless, exogenous insulin does not and probably will never equate with normal endogenous beta-cell insulin secretion. Here's why.

In a non-diabetic, the pancreatic beta cells monitor blood glucose and secrete insulin when blood glucose levels rise. The pancreas also has alpha cells, which produce glucagon, the hormone that opposes insulin and signals the liver to raise blood sugar via glycogenolysis and gluconeogenesis. When normal beta cells secrete insulin, there are two effects. First, the insulin concentration around the neighboring alpha cells rises to about one hundred times more than what occurs with exogenous insulin. The concentrated insulin acts as a feedback loop and signals the alpha cells to stop secreting glucagon. Second, the secreted insulin leaves the pancreas via the portal vein and goes directly to the liver in concentrations about three times higher than those occurring with exogenous insulin. The liver uses about half of this insulin produced to store glucose as glycogen and to suppress glycogenolysis and gluconeogenesis guided by the signal of low glucagon.

But in persons with T1DM, beta cells in the pancreas are destroyed, and only exogenous insulin is available. When insulin is injected subcutaneously, the insulin concentration around the alpha cells is only 0.01 of the normal concentration, and that reaching the liver is 0.33 of normal, so the normal feedback loop does not occur, and glucagon production is not properly regulated. This leads to abnormally high blood-glucose readings, which indicate the need for additional insulin. Alternatively, the normal response to hypoglycemia is a dramatic reduction in insulin secretion by the beta-cells and a simultaneous increase in glucagon secretion by the alpha-cells. Both of these changes signal the liver to release glucose into the blood via glycogenolysis or gluconeogenesis. In T1DM, hypoglycemia resulting from excessive exogenous insulin injection blocks the ability of the alpha-cells to secrete glucagon. There are no beta-cells left to reduce insulin secretion. Thus, the only way blood glucose can increase is for the sympathetic nervous system and adrenal glands to secrete adrenaline (epinephrine/norepinephrine), which does signal the liver to make glucose. The adrenaline also results in the symptoms of hypoglycemia, urging the person with T1DM to take a glucose tablet(s) or food quickly. A paper published in the *Journal of Clinical Investigation* titled "Glucagonocentric restructuring of diabetes" explains this in more detail.[58]

The timing and amount of absorption of exogenous insulin varies in a given individual from one injection to the next. The metabolic effect of the rapid-acting insulin aspart (Novolog) showed an intra-individual variability of between 10% and 20% in healthy volunteers in a study done at Heinrich-Heine University in Germany[59]. Heinemann et al., the authors of this paper, state the following:

> *The high variability of the metabolic response to application of identical insulin doses is a serious problem for insulin-treated diabetic patients and hampers the achievement of a good metabolic control without suffering from hypoglycemic events.*

Reason 3: Glucagon Secretion Is Not Regulated in T1DM

As mentioned above, insulin concentrations around the pancreatic alpha cells (which produce glucagon) are highly deficient in persons with T1DM, which leads to unregulated glucagon secretion and a rise in blood-glucose levels via both glycogenolysis and gluconeogenesis, particularly after meals. During a hypoglycemic episode from exogenous insulin, the blood-insulin levels are high enough to suppress glucagon secretion and interfere with what would be a normal increase in blood glucose.

Clinical trials are being conducted to test whether other medications can regulate glucagon to assist in regulating blood glucose. Another hormone, amylin, normally produced by beta cells, also helps regulate blood glucose by suppressing glucagon. In T1DM, the beta cells are destroyed, and amylin is no longer produced in the pancreas. A synthetic analog of human amylin is currently available, called Symlin (pramlintide), and is discussed later in this book. Under the influence of low insulin levels and postprandial amino-acid stimulation, the alpha cells secrete glucagon, resulting in postprandial hyperglycemia. This explains why consuming a low-carbohydrate ketogenic diet still requires a meal-time insulin bolus. The protein (i.e., amino acids) content of the meal stimulates glucagon that, in turn, stimulates hepatic glucose production.

What Can Be Done to Minimize Blood-Glucose Fluctuations?

The above discussion points out that some blood-glucose fluctuations are inherent in the current treatment of T1DM and are, therefore, beyond the control of the patient. There may come a day when other treatments alleviate these deficiencies in exogenous-insulin therapy.

Until that time, the ketogenic diet offers a rational and underutilized treatment for T1DM. By restricting carbohydrates, glucose deposits into the bloodstream are reduced, and the need for exogenous insulin and its concomitant degree of absorption variability can be reduced.

Blood-glucose fluctuations underscore the need to check blood-glucose levels frequently. Frequent checks afford the person with T1DM the opportunity to correct hypoglycemia with one or more glucose tablets and to correct hyperglycemia with small doses of rapid-acting insulin. Both blood-glucose monitoring and appropriate corrective actions are essential to help optimize glycemic control. The ketogenic diet makes this process much easier to manage.

Blood-Glucose Management Skills

In order to improve blood-sugar control, patients need to be motivated to make beneficial lifestyle- and disease-management changes. Managing diabetes is a twenty-four-hour-a-day activity. You may not need to spend more than several minutes each day doing it, but everything you eat and each physical activity in which you partake must be considered in light of their effects on your blood sugar. Under the direction of their physician, patients must be able to implement and maintain changes by themselves or with the assistance of a close family member or friend. Factors to consider include vision, manual dexterity, mental comprehension, discipline, and compliance. For example, if the patient is taking insulin and has limited sight, being physically able to inject the correct amount and type of insulin can be challenging. Mistakes in administering the amount or type of insulin can have serious adverse outcomes such as hypoglycemia. This is just one of numerous barriers to achieving improved blood glucose. Here are some of the many abilities needed to manage diabetes successfully on a ketogenic diet:

- Measure blood glucose and ketones.
- Take insulin and/or medications accurately and consistently.
- Select appropriate foods for a ketogenic diet.
- Negotiate eating outside the home in restaurants, at the homes of others, and during travel.
- Follow diet guidelines accurately and consistently.
- Have your health monitored by your physician.

We suspect that most people who are reading this book are highly motivated individuals who will follow the steps necessary to monitor and control their blood sugar. These are the individuals who can most likely achieve their target blood-glucose levels without adverse events. Imagine if 1 in 4 of the 382 million people with diabetes could achieve a much improved or normal blood glucose: there would be a tremendous reduction in suffering, disease burden, and cost of care. That would make 96 million people who would effectively have their complications of diabetes either arrested or reversed!

Using Blood-Glucose Meters

Achieving optimal blood-sugar control requires frequent blood-glucose measurements. Therefore, having one or more accurate blood-glucose meters is important. Carrying a meter at all times is recommended, especially if you are newly diagnosed or are making changes in your insulin type or dose or in your diet or exercise. Keeping an extra meter at work, at your bedside, or in the car (unless temperatures are extreme) will serve as a backup if you forget to take your meter with you. Note that the cost of a meter is relatively small compared with the cost of strips used in the meters to measure blood glucose.

Any readings that seem out of the ordinary should be rechecked after washing your hands to remove traces of food or glucose—or be rechecked with a different meter. Sometimes an unusual reading is caused by a defective glucose meter strip, but that is usually indicated by an error code. In that case, simply use a new test strip.

Some meters are more accurate than others. It is a good idea to periodically research the accuracy of currently marketed blood-glucose meters. Searching www.pubmed.gov, using the keywords "blood glucose meter accuracy comparison", should yield some helpful information. If you find a research paper that isn't available in full text, you can email the authors and sometimes they will send you the full paper.

Real-Time Continuous Glucose Monitors

A real-time continuous glucose monitor (rt-CGM) is a device with a tiny glucose sensor inserted under the skin to measure glucose levels in tissue fluid instead of blood. The device provides a glucose reading on a portable display every five minutes. Some monitors can signal an alarm for preset low or high glucose readings; others can communicate with an insulin pump and send a low-blood-glucose signal to suspend insulin-pump infusion.

Tissue-fluid readings can give a close estimate of blood glucose, but the rt-CGM can be less accurate and has been shown to lag behind when compared to blood-glucose readings. Nevertheless, it can provide valuable information, including the direction that blood-glucose levels are heading, thus providing early notification of oncoming lows and highs. In addition, it can provide information on how food, physical activity, stress, sleep, medication, and illness affect your diabetes, as well as provide estimates of glucose readings at crucial points during the day. Before making any adjustment in insulin dosage, an rt-CGM glucose reading should be confirmed with a blood-glucose meter.

An rt-CGM can be used in conjunction with an insulin pump by establishing communication between the two devices. One of the primary purposes is to suspend insulin pumping when low glucose is detected. This is especially useful while sleeping but also in other situations like driving or other activities where hypoglycemia could be dangerous.

The next iteration in this technology is to program the insulin pump to adjust the insulin infusion based on rt-CGM results. This is called an artificial pancreas. On September 28, 2016, the FDA approved the first hybrid closed loop system, the Medtronic's MiniMed 670G System, intended to automatically monitor blood sugar and adjust basal insulin doses in people with type 1 diabetes.

Do these newer technologies improve glycemic control or prevent hypoglycemia? A meta-analysis done at Johns Hopkins University and published in the Annals of Internal Medicine in 2012 examines this question. The authors made this conclusion:

> For glycemic control, rt-CGM is superior to SMBG [self-monitored blood glucose] and sensor-augmented insulin pumps are superior to MDI [multiple-dose injection] and SMBG without increasing the risk for hypoglycemia.[60]

Glycemic control as measured by HbA1c was better with rt-CGM, compared with SMBG in children with T1DM, according to a meta-analysis titled "Systematic review and meta-analysis of the effectiveness of continuous glucose monitoring (CGM) on glucose control in diabetes."[61] The results of a 2011 randomized controlled trial on the effect of CGM monitoring on hypoglycemia, by Battelino et al., showed that in both children and adults with T1DM, the time per day spent in hypoglycemia was significantly shorter in the continuous-monitoring group (rt-CGM) than it was in the control group, and there was a concomitant decrease in HbA1c.[62]

Measuring, Tracking, and Establishing Glucose Profiles

Self-monitored blood-glucose measurements should be recorded and reviewed in a log before every dose of insulin, and the log should be taken with you on visits to your doctor. This can be a simple row and column table on paper, or you can download a free blood-glucose and ketone-tracker sheet from the About This Site/Resources section on Ketogenic-Diet-Resource.com. The log should be used as an interactive tool to help determine any corrections needed to medications, insulin, or diet. This will help you improve blood-glucose control in the longer term.

Over the years, Dr. Runyan has seen patients report high blood-sugar results but fail to take any corrective actions, despite having been instructed how to do so. Worse yet, others fail to regularly measure their blood sugars. Typically, these are the patients who will have diabetic complications down the road. Knowing the misery that awaits them in the future, Dr. Runyan has been both frustrated and saddened. It's difficult to understand why some patients are unwilling to participate in their own care. Measuring blood-sugar levels solely for the purpose of documenting them is not very helpful. Instead, the results of blood-sugar measurements should be used to make adjustments to treatment (diet, exercise, or insulin) as you aim for your target blood-sugar level.

Measuring blood glucose is not difficult, and instructions are included with each glucose meter. Here are some general guidelines for testing your own blood-glucose levels. First, make sure the skin is clean and free of food, glucose, and dirt. Either side of the pad of each finger will yield blood readily, and there will be less discomfort compared with using the pad itself as is often incorrectly taught. Sometimes the thumb has thicker skin, and it should be avoided if it does not yield satisfactory results. Use locations and a lancet penetration depth that yields enough blood for your meter but is not painful.

Also, be aware that each finger has many potential areas to prick for blood glucose or ketone measurements. Some glucose meters have a special lancet device for pricking the forearm, however, readings from this location will be less accurate and are not recommended. Using the recommended locations with the correct depth of lancet insertion will provide accurate results with minimal discomfort. Lancet-insertion depths are adjustable on a five-level depth scale on most lancet devices.

Times and Reasons to Measure Blood Sugar

Below is a list of times and reasons to measure your blood sugar. Note that most are appropriate for those who take insulin or diabetic medications.

> Anytime you don't feel right and need to determine if that symptom is due to hypoglycemia.

> Upon rising, a fasting measurement is used to determine the correct evening or bedtime long-acting insulin or oral diabetes medication dose. It can also detect the dawn phenomenon: an elevation

in blood sugar due to the normal early morning rise in growth hormone and cortisol secretion in the setting of inadequate beta-cell insulin secretion.

> Before each meal, as this is used to determine the correct rapid-acting or regular mealtime insulin dose or to determine appropriate adjustments to your ketogenic diet. The insulin dose before meals is the sum of the insulin needed for the meal itself, plus or minus a corrective insulin dose, if any. This will be reviewed in more detail in chapter 9.

> After rapid-acting or regular insulin duration of action has ended. This can vary from one individual to another and from one injection site to another. The duration of action of insulin can be determined by measuring blood glucose every thirty minutes after a mealtime insulin injection. This will also be reviewed in more detail in chapter 9.

> Before and during long-term endurance exercise, and after exercise, as this will help determine how different types, intensities, and durations of exercise affect your blood sugar and your need for changes in diet, insulin, and medications. Remember, physical activities such as cutting grass, cleaning house, and gardening will count as exercise as far as your blood sugar is concerned.

> Before and periodically while driving a car or operating heavy machinery or when engaged in any activity where you or others could be injured in the event of your having hypoglycemia.

> After a correction dose of rapid-acting insulin based on the time you have determined to be the duration of action.

> Before going to bed, in case you need to correct with rapid-acting insulin or with adjustments in diet or glucose tablet(s).

> During the night, if hypoglycemia at night is a problem for you. A real-time continuous glucose monitor is also helpful in alerting you to nighttime hypoglycemia.

It's advisable to conduct a full blood-glucose profile as outlined in the steps above for an entire day for several days in a row before each doctor visit. Blood-sugar control can change for many reasons, so it's a good idea to conduct a full blood-glucose profile periodically as well. That's the nature of having diabetes. If you're not regularly checking your blood-glucose profile, then you may have either unforeseen elevated HbA1c or an increased number or severity of hypoglycemic episodes. For those on multiple insulin injections or insulin-pump therapy, the glucose profile should be a daily routine.

Please don't panic and throw up your hands in the air thinking that you have to check your blood sugar ten times each day. The number of daily blood-sugar measurements necessary to obtain and maintain optimal blood-glucose control will vary from one person to the next. In general, those taking insulin or other medications that have the potential to cause hypoglycemia will need more frequent blood-glucose measurements. That said, once you're used to measuring blood glucose frequently, and you realize how much better your blood-glucose values are because of it, we suspect you won't mind.

Finally, even if your blood-glucose meter has electronic memory and can send your readings to your and/or your doctor's computer, it is important to keep a written log of your blood glucose, ketone, and HbA1c readings and to take notes that may help you make future adjustments in diet, exercise, and other corrective measures. Notes should include the amount and type of exercise, any symptoms of hypoglycemia, the number of glucose tablets taken to correct it, and stressful or unusual situations that might affect your blood sugars, like exercise, illness, travel, or a new job. You can make your own data sheet, use a spreadsheet program to create one, or download the free blood-glucose and ketone-tracker sheet from the About This Site/Resources on ketogenic-diet-resource.com. Or you can do an Internet search for "blood-sugar log" and choose one you like.

Blood-Glucose Targets

"Target" blood glucose is the desired average blood glucose for a particular individual. Factors to consider when determining a target include motivation, age, diabetic complications, and financial and social support.

When we talk about target blood glucose, we must include both short-term and long-term goals. The short-term blood-glucose target is largely determined by the individual's current level of glycemic control. For example, if a person with poorly controlled diabetes (HbA1c of 10%, roughly equivalent to an average blood glucose of 240 mg/dL (13.3 mmol/L)) were to start a strict ketogenic diet with 30 grams of carbohydrate per day, there is a chance that this person could develop symptoms of hypoglycemia at levels of blood glucose that measure in the normal range.

The ketogenic diet can result in a rapid reduction in blood glucose during the first few days, even before keto-adaptation occurs. This person may develop the symptoms of hypoglycemia once blood glucose falls to around 100–120 mg/dL (5.6–6.7 mmol/L), which is above normal. The poorer the glycemic control (or the higher the initial HbA1c), the more likely that symptoms of hypoglycemia will be experienced. The exact reasons for this long-recognized phenomenon are not well characterized. As glycemic control improves over time, symptoms of hypoglycemia will occur at lower levels of blood glucose.

In order to minimize the likelihood of hypoglycemia in people with higher blood sugars, daily dietary carbohydrate intake can be gradually dropped over time while the insulin and/or oral diabetes medications are reduced.

The short-term blood-glucose target would also be gradually lowered over time. The short-term goal is used to help determine insulin-dose adjustments with the help of your physician. For the motivated person with fairly well controlled diabetes, (HbA1c of 6%, roughly equivalent to an average blood glucose of 126 mg/dL (7.0 mmol/L)) starting a strict ketogenic diet with 30 grams of carbohydrate per day with a near-normal blood-glucose target would be a reasonable starting point.

The time needed to reach the long-term blood-glucose target will vary from person to person. It may take several months or longer to reach that goal by adjusting insulin doses while avoiding hypoglycemia. It is more important to eventually reach your target blood glucose than to get frustrated because it hasn't been reached in some arbitrary time frame.

The ketogenic diet has the potential to rapidly reduce (not eliminate) the need for insulin in those with T1DM. It makes much more sense to work with your physician to decrease insulin in response to a reduction in dietary carbohydrates than to continue to consume carbohydrates to accommodate the insulin.

If the initial blood-glucose target is not obtainable due to hypoglycemia, inability to follow the ketogenic diet, inability to monitor blood glucose frequently enough, or for any other reason, then you should aim for a somewhat higher blood-glucose target—but still aim for as low a target as you can manage safely without having hypoglycemia.

Neither the ketogenic diet nor glycemic control of diabetes is an all-or-nothing proposition. The goal is to achieve the lowest average blood glucose that you can while avoiding hypoglycemia. For example, if you can follow a 75-gram/day carbohydrate non-ketogenic diet and achieve an average blood glucose of 100 mg/dL without hypoglycemia, and that's better than your previous markers, then your health will be much improved. Your specific blood-glucose and HbA1c targets should be discussed with your doctor as you review your blood-glucose profile and current HbA1c results.

The tables for fasting and postprandial blood-sugar ranges on the following page are meant to provide a frame of reference for target blood-glucose and HbA1c discussions with your physician.

Blood-Sugar Reference Tables

Fasting blood sugar is a measurement of your blood sugar after not eating for eight to twelve hours. This test is normally included with a comprehensive metabolic profile (CMP) test.

Fasting Blood Sugar Recommendations

Fasting blood sugars are evaluated as follows by the American Diabetes Association (ADA)[63] and the American Association of Clinical Endocrinologists (AACE).[64]

Diagnostic Criteria Based on Fasting Blood Glucose		
	ADA	AACE
Normal blood sugar range:	<100 mg/dL	<100 mg/dL
Prediabetic range:	Between 101–126 mg/dL	101–126 mg /dL
Diabetic range:	≥ 126 mg/dL (7.0 mmol/L)	≥ 126 mg/dL (7.0 mmol/L)

Postprandial Blood Sugar Recommendations

Postprandial blood sugar is a measurement of your blood sugar one to two hours after a meal. Recommendations by the ADA and the AACE are as follows:

Treatment Goals for Persons with Diabetes			
	For healthy persons	Goals for persons with diabetes	
		ADA	AACE
Blood sugars before meals:	<100 mg/dL	70–130 mg/dL	<110 mg/dL
Blood sugars two hours after meal	<120 mg/dL	<180 mg/dL	<140 mg/dL

A study titled "Variation of interstitial glucose measurements assessed by continuous glucose monitors in healthy, non-diabetic individuals" by Beck, et al., followed 74 healthy children, adolescents, and adults and found the average interstitial (similar to blood glucose) glucose over 24 hours was 98 mg/dl (5.4 mM). The diet of these individuals was not controlled or measured and it's likely they were not on a low carbohydrate diet. Average blood glucose would probably be lower on a low carbohydrate diet, but to date, there is no similar study data to confirm this. However, these individuals at the time of the study did not have metabolic syndrome, so the average glucose of 98 mg/dl is likely a healthy reading and would be a reasonable target that those with diabetes can aim.

Hypoglycemia: Symptoms and Treatment

Hypoglycemia is usually accompanied by one or more of the signs or symptoms shown below. In persons with T1DM who develop hypoglycemia as a result of taking more exogenous insulin than is currently needed (hyperinsulinemic hypoglycemia), the normal counterregulatory response of the pancreatic alpha cells to secrete glucagon is impaired. This results in loss of the normal signal to the liver to create glucose (via glycogenolysis or gluconeogenesis) when it is needed to raise blood glucose.

Hypoglycemia causes a cascade of signaling that stimulates the release of adrenalin (epinephrine and norepinephrine) and acetylcholine. These neurotransmitters and hormones help to create signals like hunger so the sufferer will seek out food/glucose to correct the problem. They also are responsible for many of the signs and symptoms of hypoglycemia:

- Confusion
- Nervousness
- Irritability

- Stubbornness
- Anxiety or panic
- Nasty behavior
- Blurred vision
- Double vision
- Unable to read or comprehend text
- Seeing spots or lights
- Visual hallucinations
- Increased hunger
- Nausea
- Restlessness
- Tiredness
- Weakness
- Rapid heartbeat
- Pounding heartbeat
- Ringing or buzzing in ears
- Sweating, feeling hot
- Sweating, feeling cold
- Headache
- Nightmares
- Appearing pale
- Dilated pupils
- Involuntary eye movement
- Slurred speech
- Convulsions/seizures
- Fainting
- Dizziness
- Lightheadedness
- Dizziness on standing
- Uncontrolled limb movements
- Clumsiness
- Difficulty walking
- Drops objects

- Inappropriate laughter
- Numbness anywhere on the body
- Tremors of hands
- Insomnia
- Awakening from sleep
- Shouting while awake or asleep
- Coma

The level to which blood glucose falls before symptoms appear depends on the degree of blood-glucose control, the frequency of hypoglycemia, and the presence or absence of keto-adaptation. Persons with T1DM with poor glycemic control will develop symptoms of hypoglycemia at a higher blood glucose compared with those with better glycemic control. Symptoms of hypoglycemia should be treated immediately with glucose, regardless of the blood-glucose reading, or the diet that the patient is following.

In addition, in a person with T1DM, or insulin-requiring T2DM for that matter, who has had numerous hypoglycemic episodes in the recent past, symptoms of hypoglycemia are diminished due to a reduced sympathetic nervous system response to epinephrine/norepinephrine. This is called *hypoglycemia unawareness* but, more accurately, is an impaired awareness of hypoglycemia with reduced symptoms.[65] This is a problem for persons with diabetes because it leads to a vicious cycle of recurrent hypoglycemia and increases the risk of severe hypoglycemia six to twenty-five fold. Severe hypoglycemia increases the risk of death from hypoglycemia, an event which occurs in up to 10% of persons with diabetes. Thus, avoiding hypoglycemia is very important, particularly if the symptoms are fewer than previously experienced.

When patients are hypoglycemic, it is common for them to go into a "panic mode." This often results in excessive consumption of sweets with subsequent hyperglycemia, and is one of the reasons why hypoglycemia is a factor in undesired weight gain and failure to achieve successful blood-sugar control.

To avoid sugar overdosing and hyperglycemia, it is preferable to use pure glucose tablets or gel (sold in grocery stores, pharmacies, and online) because these products will resolve the hypoglycemia very quickly. Table sugar will work in a pinch, but it's not the best option. The better solution is to keep a supply of glucose tablets or liquid close at hand. If you find yourself without them, anything sweetened with sugar will also work (e.g., non-diet cola, fruit juice, or candies like Smarties or SweeTARTS).

If you suspect you may be hypoglycemic, measure your blood glucose and treat yourself accordingly to bring the level up to your target using the appropriate number of glucose tablets, keeping in mind that each tablet contains four grams of glucose. It is also appropriate to take glucose tablets or sugar for suspected hypoglycemia if your glucose meter is not immediately available.

Since a normal human bloodstream only contains about five grams of glucose, you can see that hypoglycemia can be corrected with one or two tablets. It will take ten to fifteen minutes for the symptoms of hypoglycemia to resolve after consuming the glucose. If symptoms have not resolved in ten to fifteen minutes, check your blood sugar to determine whether your symptoms are due to hypoglycemia, or take additional glucose or sweets if your meter is not available. If symptoms still persist, seek medical attention. Glucose tablets do not take into account further absorption of injected insulin or the effects of oral diabetes medications, so a small snack containing protein will help prevent another drop in blood glucose during subsequent hours.

Hyperglycemia and Glycation Damage

Hyperglycemia is a condition in which excessive amounts of glucose build up in blood plasma due to either a lack of insulin or a lack of response to insulin from body tissues. A diabetic with uncontrolled blood sugars may have two to ten times the normal amount of glucose in his or her bloodstream. Excursions of blood sugar that exceed normal levels are the main cause of diabetic complications.[66]

The damage of hyperglycemia is a function of uncontrolled amounts of blood sugar being processed through cellular energy pathways. The influx of large amounts of glucose into cells increases production of reactive oxygen species (ROS), volatile compounds which can kill cells via chemical damage to cellular structures.

Elevations of ROS or "free radicals" are associated with the progression of glycation damage. Glycation is a process in which excess blood glucose bonds or "sticks" to various protein and fat molecules in body tissues. The bonding of sugar molecules causes an impairment of the glycated tissue and eventually causes extensive damage and loss of function through the formation of advanced glycation end products (AGEs). To get a good idea of how glycation works, imagine what would happen if you were to rub maple syrup on your hands and then try to fold clothes or type on a keyboard.

Measures of Glycation Damage

Measures of glycation damage are used as an estimate of hyperglycemia over time. The longer blood sugar is elevated, the more likely glycation damage will occur. A test called hemoglobin A1c (or simply HbA1c) measures hemoglobin, a protein found in red blood cells that becomes glycated when exposed to blood glucose. The longer and higher blood glucose remains above normal, the larger the percentage of hemoglobin molecules that become glycated. Measuring the amount of glycated hemoglobin gives a picture of blood-sugar levels over the past two to three months.

The composition of one's diet is closely tied to average blood-glucose values and, therefore, to HbA1c results. A study done at the Human Nutrition Research Centre at the University of Newcastle upon Tyne in the UK demonstrates the effect of starch and sugar in the diet on blood glucose in eight healthy volunteers who received a standard diet providing 55% of energy as carbohydrate, 35% as fat, and 10% as protein.

After a starch-rich meal, blood glucose peaks one hour after the meal but does not return to the pre-meal value until the following morning. After the sugar-rich meal, blood glucose peaks one hour after each meal and then it drops below the baseline two to three hours after each meal. This event is known as reactive hypoglycemia.[67]

The important point here is that the study shows that glucose levels are elevated after meals and overnight. Hence, glycation damage is more likely to occur during those times. And even though these glucose elevations after meals are temporary, they cause an elevation in average blood sugars over time. In addition, hemoglobin is not the only protein that becomes glycated during these episodes of elevated blood sugar. Numerous other proteins can be damaged by glycation. A review paper by Goldin et al. describes the consequences of glycation that occur in patients with diabetes.[68]

Glycation is one of the causes associated with complications of diabetes such as diabetic nephropathy (kidney disease and kidney failure)[69], neuropathy (nerve damage, numbness of skin, loss of body perception, Charcot foot, and muscle weakness)[70], and retinopathy (retinal hemorrhage, vitreous hemorrhage, neovascularization, blindness).[71]

And glycation damage is not limited to those with diabetes. It occurs any time blood glucose and HbA1c are persistently higher than normal, especially when inflammation is also present.

Hemoglobin A1c Test Accuracy

Physicians order glycated hemoglobin A1c tests every three to six months to monitor patient blood-glucose control with the idea that it's a rough measure of the average blood glucose over the previous two to three months. Having a substitute for average blood glucose helps physicians monitor current blood-glucose control in patients who will not check their blood glucose on a regular basis.

Although studies have suggested that there is a correlation between HbA1c and average blood glucose, and that HbA1c results can serve as a substitute for average blood glucose, self-monitored blood-glucose readings are more accurate. HbA1c test results can vary greatly from one person to another, even if people have the same average blood glucose. For example, in a 1993 paper titled "The effect of intensive treatment of diabetes on the development and progression of long-term complications in insulin-dependent diabetes mellitus," diabetics with mean plasma glucose of 214 mg/dL (11.9 mmol/L) had HbA1c results ranging from 6.2% to 12.4%, while diabetics with mean plasma glucose of 115 mg/dL (6.4 mmol/L) had HbA1c results ranging from 5.4% to 8.6%.[72]

Changes in HbA1c results over time is a useful measure of changing blood-sugar control because average blood glucose is highly correlated with individual HbA1c results. Hence, HbA1c can be of value in monitoring your progress after making a change in diet (e.g., changing to the ketogenic diet) or making a change in insulin (type or dose).

You can check your HbA1c more frequently (every three to four weeks initially) by having your own HbA1c meter. The A1c Now+ meter by Chek Diagnostics is one such meter. Keep in mind that readings from any meter will have the same value and limitations as laboratory HbA1c tests. Over time, the best way to monitor blood-glucose control is to measure your own glucose profile using your home glucose meter and track your numbers in a written or digital log.

Fructosamine

Fructosamine is a glycated molecule formed from the bonding of fructose to protein-carrier molecules in the blood (mostly albumin). Similar to HbA1c tests, a fructosamine test is designed to measure average blood glucose, but since albumin decays after fourteen to twenty-one days, the fructosamine test reflects average blood-sugar concentrations over the previous two to three weeks, instead of over months as indicated by an HbA1c.

The fructosamine test has been available through laboratories since the early 1980s. It's useful for monitoring a dietary or medication adjustment to correct blood glucose quickly, especially during pregnancy. It's also useful in patients with genetic defects that result in an abnormal structure within red-blood-cell hemoglobin molecules where the hemoglobin A1c test results might be misleading. In patients with shortened red-blood-cell lifespans, fructosamine is thought to be more reliable than the HbA1c test.[73] These conditions include kidney disease, liver disease, hemolytic anemia, HIV, iron-deficiency anemia, and aplastic anemia.

The interpretation of fructosamine depends upon the individual's age and sex. The table below gives the diagnostic ranges. Because of the significant overlap in these ranges, the relative change in fructosamine over time is more valuable than the absolute number.

Population	Fructosamine range
Non-diabetic individuals	175 to 280 mmol/L
Diabetics with controlled blood sugars	210 to 421 mmol/L
Diabetics with uncontrolled blood sugars	268 to 870 mmol/L

Troubleshooting Elevated Blood Glucose

Lowering blood sugar and increasing ketone levels can be difficult even when following a strict ketogenic diet. Here are some points to consider if you are having trouble getting your baseline blood-sugar levels to drop.

> *Physical stress:* Diabetes is a metabolic source of stress. Just trying to control your blood sugar becomes a source of worry and stress-generated aberrations.

> *Mental stress:* Excess emotional stress can increase levels of cortisol, a hormone that can increase blood sugar. Find ways to decrease emotional and mental stress. Try yoga, prayer, meditation, art projects, or doing something that you love that absorbs your attention and takes your mind off of your health.

> *Medications:* Some medications such as barbiturates, diuretics, catecholamines, and antipsychotics can increase blood sugar. Talk

to your primary-care physician about alternatives if this becomes an issue. A list of 390 drugs that can affect your blood sugar is available at www.diabetesincontrol.com.[74]

> *Protein consumption:* It is very easy to "overeat" protein if food intake is not tracked via a food scale and log. At each meal, most people only need a serving of meat about the size of a deck of playing cards. To determine if too much protein is raising your blood sugar, try lowering your daily protein intake by ten grams and track how your blood sugar responds. Ten grams equates to about 1.25 ounces less protein each day.

> *Hidden carbs:* Read labels and count every carbohydrate in food, drinks, and supplements. Sugar alcohols and hidden fillers in foods can cause blood sugar to rise and interfere with ketosis for some people.

> *Carbohydrate intake on food labels:* Food labels do not provide accurate measures of carbohydrate. Food manufacturers can list zero carbohydrates for up to 0.5 grams of carbohydrate per serving.

> *Vitamins, fish oil, herbal supplements:* These can have hidden carbs. In addition, taking large amounts of fish oil can drive up blood sugar. You may have to eliminate your supplements for several days while monitoring blood sugar. Reintroduce them one at a time to determine which one might be the source of trouble.

> *Caffeine intake:* Drinking caffeinated coffee or sugar-free cocoa or eating dark chocolate and other foods containing caffeine can drive up blood sugar.

> *Low thyroid function:* Check with your doctor on your thyroid status.

> *Caloric intake:* Use a base metabolic rate (BMR) calorie calculator to find the recommended caloric intake for your goal weight, and adjust your caloric intake to match.[75] If you are losing weight that you don't want to lose, eat more protein, fat, or both.

> *Exercise:* Moderate exercise can elevate blood sugar for a short time right afterward, however, it reduces baseline blood sugar and insulin needs in the long run. In contrast, vigorous exercise can raise blood sugar for longer periods due to a stress response.

> *Micronutrients:* Deficiencies of micronutrients, such as magnesium and chromium, can be detrimental to blood-sugar control. Taking at least a basic multi-vitamin/multi-mineral each day is recommended. Vitamin D levels should also be checked and optimized. See the supplement recommendations in appendix A.

> *Colds, flu, and other illnesses:* Fighting off a viral or bacterial infection like a cold or the flu will result in elevated blood sugars. In addition, most cold medications are laced with some type of sugar. It's a good idea to search out cold and flu medications that are carbohydrate free and stock up. Ask your pharmacist to assist you.

> *Menstrual cycles:* Women should be aware that the onset of menstruation also elevates blood sugar for a few days.

> *Age in general:* Younger people will generally respond better to dietary changes with faster drops in blood sugar and higher ketone levels, often within days of starting the diet. Older people will find this process takes longer.

> *Consistency of meal macronutrients:* It is important to keep the macronutrient (protein, fat, and carbs) amounts and ratios consistent at each meal from day to day. This makes predicting insulin dose needs and blood glucose response much more consistent from day to day.

Monitoring Ketone Levels

When following a ketogenic diet, monitoring urine, blood, or breath ketones can provide useful information about whether you are in a state of nutritional ketosis. Why is this important? Monitoring ketones can provide some assurance that you are following the ketogenic diet correctly and that a state of nutritional ketosis has been achieved.

Measuring urine ketones is the least expensive way to monitor nutritional ketosis. Bayer Ketostix is one such product. Ketone strips detect acetoacetate in urine and range from trace (<5 mg/dL) to large (160 mg/dL). When beginning the ketogenic diet, it may take several days for urine ketones to rise above trace amounts. Moderate to large urine-ketone levels (40–160 mg/dL) are consistent with nutritional ketosis. It is important to keep in mind that the absence of dark pink or purple on your urine test strips does not necessarily mean that your body isn't generating ketones. Many factors can affect the concentration of acetone in the urine throughout the day. After months on a ketogenic diet, a minority of individuals can be in nutritional ketosis yet have only trace amounts of urine ketones due to improved renal reabsorption of ketones.[76] While in a state of nutritional ketosis, urine ketones could be temporarily at a trace level if your water intake is higher than average. Alternatively, urine-ketone levels could be higher (160 mg/dL) because of low fluid intake or fluid loss from sweating, vomiting, or diarrhea. Dehydration acts to concentrate urine, which increases urine-ketone concentration. Persistently negative urine ketones can also reflect an absence of nutritional ketosis due to excessive carbohydrate or protein intake or both.

Ketones measured in urine were noted to be reflective of changes in serum, and this led to the adoption of urine-ketone measurement as a standard method for determining the degree of ketosis induced by a ketogenic diet. But blood ketones are still a valuable tool. For example, if you have had positive urine ketones in the past, and, without a change in your ketogenic diet, your urine ketones become persistently negative, measuring blood ketones can help determine the cause. When you have negative urine ketones but your blood ketones are in excess of 0.5 mM, the kidneys may have improved their ability to retain ketones—to the point that measuring urine ketones will no longer be a useful test for you. However, if you have negative urine ketones and your blood ketones are less than 0.5 mM, this means that the ketones actually are low, indicating that you are not in nutritional ketosis. Your diet has changed enough to stop ketosis, and you should reassess your carbohydrate and protein intake.

A blood-ketone meter, like Abbott Laboratories' Precision Xtra, measures the concentration of a ketone called beta-hydroxybutyrate (BHOB) in millimoles per liter (mmole/liter or mM). Nutritional ketosis is defined as having levels of blood BHOB in the range of 0.5–3 mM per the recommendation of Jeff Volek, RD, PhD, and Stephen Phinney, MD, PhD. Note that blood-ketone levels vary during the course of the day, with higher readings in the afternoon.[77]

Whether it is better to have a blood BHOB concentration closer to 3 mM than to 0.5 mM when treating diabetes is not clear at this point. Based on studies of fasting humans[78], the brain oxidation of ketones increases linearly as the blood-ketone levels increase to 4 mM. Brain oxidation of ketones levels off as blood-ketone levels increase above 4 mM total ketone body concentration. A total ketone body concentration of 4 mM corresponds to a BHOB concentration of 3 mM. Thus, it is theoretically possible that the brain could be protected from hypoglycemia, at least partially, by having blood BHOB concentrations closer to 3 mM than to 0.5 mM. This needs to be studied in persons with T1DM on a ketogenic diet. The primary determinate of blood BHOB concentration is the degree of carbohydrate restriction: fewer dietary carbohydrates translates to more ketones. The secondary determinate is dietary protein intake: less protein intake translates to more ketones. Although there is no dietary requirement for carbohydrates, you do need protein in a range of 1.0–1.5 grams/kg BW/day. Also, remember than there are foods that are beneficial and nutrient-dense that contain small amounts of carbohydrate and should be included in a ketogenic diet. A ketogenic diet for diabetes should be low in carbohydrates but not necessarily absent of carbohydrates.

The Ketonix meter measures acetone in the breath. Acetone is a spontaneous by-product of acetoacetate, one of the ketones produced by the liver during nutritional ketosis. Ketonix was developed by an engineer in Sweden, Michel Lundell, who wanted an easier method to monitor his own nutritional ketosis for treatment of epilepsy. It is a one-time expense, but it can be used hundreds of times, making it quite cost effective. Ketonix is also easy and convenient to use since you simply exhale into the device, and no blood or urine is needed. It has not been independently tested against blood or urine measurements so each individual needs to make his or her own correlation between its percentage (0–100%) readout and your personal therapeutic goals. By way of disclosure, a Ketonix device was gifted to Dr. Runyan by Michel Lundell. Dr. Runyan has posted his results using this device on his blog at ketogenicdiabeticathlete.wordpress.com.

9

Insulin: Action, Peak, and Duration

Humans cannot live without insulin. For those with T1DM, with the exception of a short "honeymoon" period that sometimes occurs, insulin via injection or pump is necessary for life. As we explore the use of insulin for treating T1DM in this chapter, keep in mind that you should not change your insulin therapy without consulting with your doctor.

For all practical purposes, the primary difference between various insulin preparations is the onset of action, time to peak action, and the duration of action.

- *Onset of action* is the length of time after injection that it takes for insulin to reach your bloodstream and begin to lower blood glucose.

- *Time to peak action* is the time after injection when insulin is at its "peak" or maximum effectiveness at lowering blood glucose.

- *Duration of action* is the length of time after injection that insulin continues to lower blood glucose.

This is important to understand because by using more than one type of insulin by injection, blood glucose can be controlled to near-normal levels around the clock.

The terms *basal insulin* and *bolus insulin* refer to their functions in the treatment of insulin-requiring diabetes. The role of basal insulin is to keep blood-glucose levels at consistent levels during periods between meals and overnight. Bolus insulin is a dose specifically taken at meal times to keep blood-glucose levels under control following a meal.

When treating insulin-requiring diabetes (either T1DM or T2DM) with exogenous (injected) insulin, the goal is to mimic the natural insulin-secreting pattern of the pancreas. Since pancreatic insulin is secreted on a minute-to-minute basis, and exogenous insulin is injected into subcutaneous fat, the two cannot be identical in effect. (See reason 2 under the section titled "Why Blood Glucose Is So Variable for Type 1 Diabetics" in chapter 8 for more details.) However, with the use of insulin analogs, endogenous-insulin effects can be approximated with exogenous insulin.

> Long-acting insulin analogs such as glargine (Lantus), detemir (Levemir), degludec U200 (Tresiba), and glargine U300 (Toujeo) mimic basal pancreatic-insulin secretion. Long-acting insulin enters the bloodstream one to two hours after injection and may be effective for as long as twenty-four hours. The newer basal insulin analogs, degludec U200 and glargine U300, have durations of action of 42 and >30 hours, respectively.

> Rapid-acting lispro (Humalog), aspart (Novolog), and glulisine (Apidra) and short-acting regular insulin (Humulin Regular and Novulin Regular) mimic bolus pancreatic-insulin secretion that occurs during and after meals.

> Rapid-acting insulin begins to effect blood glucose about fifteen minutes after injection. While rapid-acting insulins may peak in an hour, they continue to work up to 5 hours. Rapid-acting insulin should be injected before a meal if blood glucose is normal or high or after the meal if blood glucose is low. It's important to postpone injecting a rapid-acting insulin until the meal is available and ready to eat. In other words, don't inject insulin on the promise of

a meal coming; wait until it actually arrives. This will help avoid hypoglycemia.

> Short-acting regular insulin has an onset of action of 1/2 hour to 1 hour, peak effect in 2 to 4 hours, and duration of action of 6 to 8 hours.

In addition, rapid-acting mealtime insulin is used as the bolus insulin for most individuals who have normal stomach (gastric) emptying time and therefore a normal rate of nutrient absorption. For those with delayed gastric emptying from diabetic gastroparesis, short-acting regular insulin is used as the bolus insulin since it will prevent postprandial hypoglycemia from the mismatch between rapid insulin absorption and the delayed nutrient absorption caused by diabetic gastroparesis. We've provided a table that compares different insulin preparations (see the bottom of the "About This Site/Resources" page of the ketogenic-diet-resource.com website to download it). Information presented in the table has been adapted from a document found online at camdenhealth.org.[79]

Consult with your physician to see if the instructions in the table might be right for you. Again, never change the manner in which you take insulin without first consulting with your doctor.

NPH Insulin

NPH insulin (Humulin N, Novolin N, Novolin NPH, NPH Iletin II, and isophane insulin) has three potential problems compared to the newer basal insulin analogs.

First, the protamine that is added to human insulin to make NPH can cause major life-threatening allergic reactions in some individuals if they receive protamine to reverse the effects of heparin (an anticoagulant) after various medical procedures.[80]

Second, because NPH insulin has a peak of action in the middle of the night when it is injected as long-acting insulin at dinnertime or bedtime, it can cause nighttime hypoglycemia more often than the long-acting basal insulin analogs.[81]

And third, NPH has an inconsistent absorption rate when injected subcutaneously, which makes glycemic control less predictable. There are many reasons for the variability of absorption rate; however, an important reason is that NPH is a suspended crystalline insulin rather than a soluble insulin.

Premixed insulin preparations contain both NPH and either regular or rapid-acting insulin in different fixed ratios. Mixing NPH with other insulins affects the bioavailability and variability of biphasic insulin mixtures. More importantly, to get optimal blood-glucose control, patients need flexibility in choosing the correct basal and bolus insulin doses rather than having a fixed basal to bolus ratio. The analog basal insulins glargine (Lantus), detemir (Levemir), Tresiba (degludec U200), and Toujeo (glargine U300) lack the above mentioned potential problems, but note that they cannot be mixed with any other insulins and, thus, require separate injections.

We refer you to a review article titled "Bioavailability and variability of biphasic insulin mixtures" for a detailed discussion of other reasons for the variable degree of absorption and variable absorption rate of NPH insulin and NPH insulin mixtures.[82]

Carbohydrate Counting Doesn't Work

Both T1DM and T2DM individuals are taught to count carbohydrates while consuming a diet containing 45%–65% of energy from carbohydrates, particularly if they are taking insulin, trying to address hypoglycemic episodes, or trying to improve poor glycemic control. Most individuals find that this strategy is not very effective in achieving any of these goals and often blame themselves for their lack of success. It turns out this self-blame is misplaced, as there are much more logical reasons for this lack of success.

The carbohydrate-counting method is based on a linear model. Using this linear model, each individual is supposed to determine how many units of insulin to inject for the number of grams of carbohydrate consumed. For example, you might initially determine that you need 1 unit of insulin for 20 grams of dietary carbohydrate. So, if your meal contains 80 grams of dietary carbohydrate, then you take 4 units of insulin. A study done by Marran et al. and published in The South African Medical Journal showed that this simple linear calculation is not based in reality.[83] Using the linear carbohydrate-to-insulin ratio (carbohydrate counting) currently recommended by ADA and AACE, the study showed an exponential increase in after-meal blood-glucose excursions with increasing carbohydrate loads. Reasons for this exponential increase center on three variables:

1. Counting carbohydrate grams does not account for great variation in the actual amount of glucose absorbed from various carbohydrate-containing foods.

2. There is variation in the amount of insulin that gets absorbed from an injection site.

3. If protein content varies from meal to meal, it could throw off the results.

The combination of these variables largely explains why carbohydrate counting on a standard high-carbohydrate diet does not work for estimating insulin dosage. This may also help explain why choosing foods based on glycemic load while eating a higher-carb diet is not effective in achieving normal glycemic control. Several other studies have confirmed that the linear carbohydrate-to-insulin-ratio method is ineffective.

A meta-analysis of studies published in The Lancet titled "Efficacy of carbohydrate counting in type 1 diabetes" examined the effectiveness of carbohydrate counting in T1DM and reported:

> "We identified seven eligible trials, of 311 potentially relevant studies, comprising 599 adults and 104 children with type 1 diabetes. Study quality score averaged 7.6 out of 13. Overall there was no significant improvement in HbA1c

concentration with carbohydrate counting versus the control or usual care."[84]

A randomized controlled trial of 281 patients with type 2 diabetes done by Bergenstal et al. was designed to test the effect of carbohydrate counting on HbA1c compared to a standard insulin adjustment algorithm. The authors found there was no significant difference in HbA1c between the simple algorithm versus carb counting.[85]

In the GIOCAR study by Laurenzi et al., 56 persons with T1DM using an insulin pump were followed. One group of 26 were assigned to carbohydrate counting while 26 controls continued their usual management. At 24 weeks, the intention-to-treat group, showed no significant difference between their HbA1c, hypoglycemic and hyperglycemic episodes and fasting blood-glucose values.[57]

Protein and Fat in Meals

In persons on a ketogenic diet, insulin dosages should also be adjusted to address the protein and fat content of each meal. Therefore, it is helpful to keep the content of all the macronutrients (carbohydrate, protein, and fat) of each meal as constant as possible from day to day. For example, daily breakfast choices should have about the same number of carbohydrate, protein, and fat grams. Breakfast macronutrients need not necessarily equal lunch or dinner, but they should be similar to breakfast yesterday.

Insulin Injection Techniques

Even though insulin doses will be lower while on the ketogenic diet, it's a good idea to rotate injections to different locations within your chosen body area to avoid the possibility of fat hypertrophy, a lump under the skin caused by accumulation of extra fat at the site of many subcutaneous injections of insulin. Below are some helpful injection techniques to follow:

> ➤ The areas chosen for injection should have some subcutaneous fat. Pinching up the skin before injecting can prevent it from going into muscle if there isn't much subcutaneous fat. Injecting into muscle will accelerate the rate of insulin absorption and would typically be desirable only for treating high blood sugar with rapid-acting insulin. If you can't pinch up some skin, avoid that area because there is not enough fat in that location.

> ➤ Using a shorter needle (6 mm) will also help prevent injecting into muscle.

> ➤ Skin should be cleaned but alcohol swabs are not necessary.

> ➤ To minimize discomfort, insert the needle quickly. Slow insertion of the needle is more painful than rapid insertion.

> ➤ Sometimes a drop of blood will appear on the skin after removing the needle. Just apply mild pressure with a paper napkin, and it will stop bleeding in a few seconds. Should you get blood on your clothing, hydrogen peroxide will remove it.

> ➤ Sometimes a small amount of insulin will leak out of the injection site. The amount that leaks out is so small it is unlikely to make much difference. Removing the needle more slowly after injection can sometimes decrease or stop the leakage. Removing the needle slowly is not painful.

Insulin Pumps

Insulin pumps are an option for insulin-requiring diabetes. Insulin pumps are programmable devices that inject either rapid-acting or regular insulin into subcutaneous fat as a bolus for meals or to correct elevated blood sugar. They also provide a continuous infusion to mimic pancreatic basal-insulin secretion at an adjustable rate that is programmed by the user. Typically, rapid-acting insulin is used in order to more closely mimic pancreatic-insulin secretion.

Because insulin doses are significantly smaller (typically half) on a ketogenic diet, it's important to choose an insulin pump that is able to deliver insulin at a rate compatible with your needs. For example, the OmniPod system can deliver insulin in increments of 0.05 units/hr while the smallest increment others deliver is 0.1 units/hr.

Other brands of insulin pumps include the One Touch Ping and MiniMed 530G. An insulin pump and real-time continuous glucose monitor (rt-CGMs) can be used at the same time, but because the rt-CGMs are not accurate enough to be used to determine insulin therapy, this combination has not been used as an artificial pancreas. On a side note, on September 28, 2016, the FDA approved the first hybrid closed loop system (artificial pancreas), the Medtronic's MiniMed 670G System, intended to automatically monitor blood sugar and adjust basal insulin doses in people with type 1 diabetes.

The MiniMed 530G with Enlite Sensor combines an insulin pump and rt-CGM, which communicates readings to the pump and can suspend the pump at a set low-glucose reading. It can also issue alerts for both low- and high-glucose readings. This is an especially useful feature during sleep.

There are potential complications related to insulin-pump use. These include hyperglycemia, hypoglycemia, diabetic ketoacidosis related to pump or tubing malfunction, infection at the catheter site, and scar tissue at the insulin infusion site. It is recommended that insulin-pump users have insulin syringes and long-acting insulin available in the event of pump failure.

For some individuals, insulin pumps are advisable and can result in improved glycemic control with limited risk of adverse events. In a study by Johnson et al., which examined the long-term outcomes of insulin pump therapy in type 1 children, "a total of 345 patients on pump therapy were matched to controls on injections. The mean HbA1c reduction in the pump cohort was 0.6% (6.6 mmol/mol). This improved HbA1c remained significant throughout the 7 years of follow-up. Pump therapy reduced severe hypoglycemia from 14.7 to 7.2

events per 100 patient-years."[86] That is not to say that insulin-pump therapy is superior for all persons with T1DM. Very effective results can be obtained with multiple dose injections as well. The mode of insulin administration is an individual decision that should be discussed with your physician.

Insulin Therapy for Type 1 Diabetes Mellitus

Insulin is necessary to treat T1DM. Without insulin therapy, the person with T1DM will have uncontrolled high blood glucose, hyperglycemic glycosuria (glucose in urine) leading to frequent urination and thirst, weight loss from both fat and muscle loss, various short- and long-term complications, and eventually die, regardless of which diet they follow. With insulin therapy, the closer exogenous insulin treatment can mimic endogenous insulin secretion, the fewer long-term complications will occur. Thus, the goal of insulin therapy is to achieve glycemic control as close to the nondiabetic range as can be accomplished safely (i.e., while avoiding hypoglycemia).

This goal is best achieved with a combination of long-acting basal insulin and rapid-acting or regular mealtime insulin. Since most persons consume three meals daily, three insulin injections would be needed for meals, and depending on the basal insulin used and one's response to it, another one or two insulin injections would be necessary.

Insulin therapy is intensive because it requires multiple daily insulin injections (MDII) and blood-glucose readings daily. The best way to handle this is to decide that insulin injections are no big deal. As explained above, insulin needles currently available are very small (31 or 32 gauge). If you use proper injection techniques, they are virtually painless.

Another option that achieves equivalent results is a continuous subcutaneous insulin infusion (CSII) pump that is often combined with real-time continuous glucose monitoring (rt-CGM). When combined with a ketogenic diet, intensive insulin therapy can improve glycemic control while reducing hypoglycemia and preventing long-term complications.

Basal-Insulin Therapy

Basal-insulin therapy is used to mimic the continuous pancreatic beta-cell secretion needed to facilitate glucose, protein, and fat regulation between meals, during the overnight fast, and during prolonged fasting as might occur in unusual circumstances. This can also be accomplished with an insulin pump that uses a rapid-acting insulin such as lispro (Humalog), aspart (Novolog), glulisine (Apidra), or regular insulin. The injectable basal-insulin preparations are glargine (Lantus), detemir (Levemir), degludec U200 (Tresiba), and glargine U300 (Toujeo). Degludec U200 and glargine U300 are given once daily. Lantus is given once daily, but it can be given twice daily if that improves glucose control. Levemir is approved for either once or twice daily, however, the pharmacodynamics of Levemir are different from Lantus, as shown in a study by Plank et al. The authors reported the following:

> *Duration of action for insulin detemir was dose dependent and varied from 5.7, to 12.1, to 19.9, to 22.7, to 23.2 hours for 0.1, 0.2, 0.4, 0.8, and 1.6 units/kg, respectively.*[87]

This is important to understand because the duration of action decreases as the Levemir dose decreases as a result of the ketogenic diet. Therefore, a person on a ketogenic diet may find that the effect of once-daily Levemir wears off before 24 hours. For example, if a 150 lb. person (68 kg) takes 14 units of Levemir once daily, the duration of action according to this study would be 12.1 hours (14 units/68 kg = 0.2 units/kg Levemir). The effect of Levemir would wear off 12 hours sooner than expected and would likely result in an increase in blood glucose. Giving Levemir twice daily would prevent this increase in blood glucose.

Whether you give the evening basal-insulin dose at dinner or bedtime is determined by glycemic control during the night and in the morning. Some persons with a significant rise in blood sugar in the early morning hours (dawn phenomenon) find a bedtime dose more effective in suppressing early morning hepatic-glucose production due to the normal early morning rise in cortisol and growth hormone compared to a dinnertime dose. Similarly, some may find a dinnertime dose more effective in preventing nighttime hypoglycemia compared to a bedtime dose.

Most individuals can be taught to titrate their own insulin dose. Basal-insulin dosing can be adjusted up or down by 1 to 2 units no more frequently than once or twice a week due to the long half-life of basal insulin. Of course, the dose must be decreased if nighttime, morning, or between-meal hypoglycemia develops.

A correct basal-insulin dose allows a meal to be skipped if needed without resulting in either hypoglycemia or hyperglycemia. For those on an insulin pump, the basal-insulin rate serves the purpose of a basal-insulin injection and provides more flexibility in adjustment when conditions, such as the level of exercise, change. This is one advantage of insulin-pump therapy.

Mealtime Insulin Therapy

Most meals will require a dose of rapid-acting or regular mealtime insulin. Even on a ketogenic diet, the protein, fat, and small amount of carbohydrate in a meal requires that insulin be available to metabolize the food and maintain glycemic control. It may be tempting to skip the mealtime insulin dose due to its much smaller size, however, this can result in several hours of elevated blood glucose after each meal. This can be avoided with small mealtime insulin doses and appropriate basal-insulin doses. Of course, there may be times when not taking mealtime insulin on a ketogenic diet is appropriate, for example, if one has low blood glucose before a meal and plans to exercise shortly afterward or finished exercising earlier.

A check of blood glucose before each meal is used to determine the correct dose of rapid-acting or regular mealtime insulin (or "bolus" with an insulin pump). The dose of mealtime insulin on a ketogenic diet will generally be significantly lower than when one is on a high-carbohydrate diet. Your doctor will likely advise you to start with a low dose, say 1 to 2 units for average-sized adults, less for children, or more for large adults, and then adjust up or down over time. The total insulin dose chosen before meals is the insulin needed for the meal itself, plus or minus a corrective insulin dose, if any.

For example, if your target blood glucose is 96 mg/dL and your pre-meal blood glucose is 149 mg/dL, you will need a larger mealtime insulin dose. If your rapid-acting insulin dose for dinner is 3 units, and you have estimated that a corrective dose factor of rapid-acting insulin will lower your blood glucose 30 mg/dL per unit of insulin, your mealtime insulin dose will be 4.75 units (3 + (149 − 96)/30 = 4.75 units).

Similarly, if your pre-meal blood glucose is 73 mg/dL, you will need a smaller mealtime insulin dose. In this example, you calculate 3 + (73 − 96)/30 = 2.25 units. It's prudent to err on the side of less insulin in cases where blood glucose is already low. In this example, the mealtime insulin dose would be 2 units. Note that this calculation assumes a constant linear relationship between the amount of insulin administered and the resulting blood glucose, which is not necessarily the case. It is an approximation at best. You can always give a correction insulin dose a few hours after the meal, if needed, but avoiding hypoglycemia is the highest priority.

The correction dose factor of 30 mg/dL per unit of insulin in the above example is not necessarily a constant. It can vary with time of day, insulin sensitivity related to current levels of exercise, changes in body weight, and the current level of blood glucose, which is nonlinear. Therefore, you should reassess the correction factor frequently.

An example of nonlinear glucose lowering is seen when 1 unit of rapid-acting insulin lowers blood glucose from 120 to 90 mg/dL (a reduction of 30 mg/dL), but the same dose only lowers it from 200 to 180 mg/dL (a reduction of 20 mg/dL). Keeping a written log of blood glucose and noting the effect of corrective doses of insulin at times when food is not being consumed can help determine your current correction factor.

Short-acting regular insulin (Humulin Regular and Novulin Regular), having a slower onset and peak action, is often used as mealtime insulin instead of rapid-acting insulin to prevent hypoglycemia for those with diabetic gastroparesis (delayed stomach emptying due to autonomic neuropathy). This is due to the fact that rapid-acting insulin can have its effect in lowering blood glucose faster than the protein and carbohydrate in a ketogenic meal can raise blood glucose. After a meal it is important to have blood glucose return to your target level at the time when mealtime insulin has been completely absorbed. For rapid-acting insulin this absorption time can vary from two to five hours, depending on the person, site of injection, dose injected, and timing of exercise.

You see how many aspects of diabetes care are contextual. Over time, the various factors involved will be become apparent from measuring your blood glucose.

T1DM Insulin-Management Skills: An Example

We will use Jack as our example patient to illustrate several diabetes management skills. Jack has been a normal weight T1DM patient (80 kg = 176 lb.) for the past fifteen years. He and his physician have decided that his target blood glucose should be 96 mg/dL. He chooses to eat two meals a day, breakfast and dinner, because he's busy at work and never seems to be hungry at lunchtime on his ketogenic diet. He takes Lantus 7 units with breakfast and dinner, but he knows he can change his dose when needed. He takes Humalog injections at mealtimes.

Jack wants to determine his mealtime insulin duration of action so he will know when to check his blood glucose after his Humalog injection. He measures his fasting blood glucose before breakfast at 96 mg/dL and eats his usual breakfast containing 15 grams of total carbohydrate from olives and an ounce each of Brazil nuts, macadamia nuts, and pumpkin seeds. He gets a total of 55 grams of protein by including an additional six ounces of salmon, and he rounds out his fat intake by drinking unsweetened coffee with 2 tablespoons of coconut oil.

At 1.5 hours after injection of 2 units of Humalog, his blood glucose is 133 mg/dL; at 2 hours after injection, his blood glucose is 113 mg/dL; at 2.5 hours after injection, his blood glucose is 93 mg/dL; at 3 hours after injection, his blood glucose is 95 mg/dL. Seeing that his blood glucose has leveled off, he concludes that the duration of action of Humalog is 2.5 hours. He now knows that 2.5 hours after each Humalog injection at breakfast, he should check his blood gl96ucose. If his basal-insulin dose is correct, then his next pre-meal blood glucose should remain constant. This duration of action test could be repeated after dinner the following day as well. Should his weight, insulin requirement, exercise regimen, body site of insulin injections, or protein or carbohydrate composition of breakfast change significantly, then repeating this test may be necessary.

Since there are so many variables involved in managing diabetes, keeping as many of them as constant as possible will help you achieve your target blood glucose. One of the variables pertinent to mealtime insulin is diet. Keeping protein and carbohydrate content constant (and the carb content low, of course) at each meal will help you achieve your target blood glucose. Taking about twenty to thirty grams of protein at each meal or evenly dividing daily protein intake between each meal also helps maintain lean muscle mass.[88]

Now let's return to our T1DM patient, Jack, and go through a day of insulin and glucose management while eating a ketogenic diet. He notes his fasting blood glucose is 96 mg/dL and blood ketone level is 1.5 mM, both of which are right on target. He has his usual salmon, olives, nuts, and seeds for breakfast. Jack decides to take 2 units of Humalog by injection. Now, 2.5 hours after breakfast, his blood glucose is 132 mg/dL. Assuming his basal-insulin dose is correct and he does nothing additional (e.g., exercise), his blood glucose would remain about the same at 132 mg/dL until the next meal. But because Jack chooses to eat two meals a day, his blood glucose would remain elevated for about 11 hours until dinner. Instead, he decides to take a corrective dose of rapid-acting insulin. As with any new insulin-dose decision, he starts low and adjusts later doses based on previous responses. This is why keeping a record of all blood-glucose readings and insulin doses is important, and Jack is glad he does that.

Jack calculates that his blood glucose is elevated by 132 − 96 = 36 mg/dL and decides to take 1 unit of Humalog. His blood glucose 2.5 hours later is 88 mg/dL, close enough to his target. Now he can use this to calculate that 1 unit of Humalog lowers his blood glucose by 132 − 88 = 44 mg/dL. He makes note of this correction factor, but he knows that this could change in the future due to a change in weight, exercise, stress, other medications (e.g., corticosteroids) or, sometimes, for unexplained reasons. Most people who have had diabetes for some time know that things keep changing. Managing diabetes well means being alert to changes so that an appropriate response can be made.

Jack finishes work at 4:00 pm and meets a friend at the gym for a game of racquetball. He checks his blood glucose before the game, its 93 mg/dL. Jack plays a pretty intense game with quite a few sprints for the ball. He feels fine but checks his blood glucose because he is driving home: it's 148 mg/dL. He concludes that the hormones released during exercise caused the increase in blood glucose, but his drive home is short so he does not take any insulin. By the time he gets home, it's 6:30 pm, time for dinner. Jack's pre-meal blood glucose is 140 mg/dL. He tries to keep his dinner carbohydrates and protein about the same each night. For dinner, he's planning to have a 6-ounce grilled beef patty with 2 tablespoons of Worcestershire sauce. He has a dinner plate full of non-starchy cooked vegetables (broccoli, bok choy, collard greens) with 2 tablespoons of butter. For dessert, he has 1 ounce each of macadamia nuts and pumpkin seeds, and unsweetened coffee with 3 tablespoons heavy whipping cream.

He estimates that, due to the extra grams of carbohydrates in the non-starchy vegetables at dinner, his Humalog dose should be 3 units.

He decides to add a correction dose due to his elevated blood glucose of 140 mg/dL. He uses his Humalog dose correction factor of 44 mg/dL per unit of insulin as follows: (140 − 96)/44 = 1 unit Humalog, and takes 3 + 1 = 4 units of insulin at the start of dinner. His dinner macronutrient totals are 25 grams of total carbohydrate from his non-starchy vegetables, Brazil nuts, and macadamia nuts, and 50 grams of protein primarily from his six-ounce beef patty and nuts. His daily totals come to: 118 grams protein (or 1.5 grams/kg body weight), 40 grams total carbohydrate, and 190 grams fat.

His macronutrient calorie ratios are 20% protein, 7% carbohydrate, and 73% fat, and he's keenly aware that the grams of protein and carbohydrate consumed are what's most important to track because they have a greater effect on blood sugar. Jack normally does not track his intake this closely, however, if he knows the nutritional composition of his diet, it can certainly be helpful if he has to diagnose a problem with high blood sugar or weight gain. Jack is also not concerned about the amount of saturated fat (SFA) he eats for two reasons.

First, he is in nutritional ketosis and that means he's a prodigious fat burner. Saturated and monounsaturated fats are burned preferentially while in nutritional ketosis. In a study by Volek and Phinney et al., the authors demonstrated that subjects on a ketogenic diet had a larger drop in serum saturated-fat levels after twelve weeks on a ketogenic diet despite consuming more than three times as much saturated fat compared to subjects on a low-fat diet.[89]

Second, Jack knows that 56 of the 190 grams of fat in his meals came from coconut oil, which is mostly saturated fat. In addition, coconut oil is a special fat that contains medium-chain triglycerides that are delivered straight to the liver and largely converted to ketones while in nutritional ketosis. It is not unusual that adding coconut oil to a ketogenic diet results in a significant increase in blood ketone levels in 3 to 4 hours. Jack checks his blood glucose 2.5 hours after dinner and finds his reading is 65 mg/dL. He decides to take one glucose tablet containing 4 grams of pure glucose. Fifteen minutes later, he rechecks his blood glucose to be sure of the reading before going to bed: its 98 mg/dL. He takes some cheese or other protein-containing snack to prevent recurrence of hypoglycemia in light of his exercise. He's thrilled with his results but makes note of the possibility that his hypoglycemia was due to the 1 unit corrective dose of Humalog at dinner that he apparently did not need due to the improved insulin sensitivity from his racquetball game in the afternoon. He also notes that this improved insulin sensitivity will last for 16 to 72 hours after the exercise.[90,91] Jack records all of his exercise sessions, blood glucose, ketone levels, and insulin doses in his log to aid in his glycemic management.

The above scenario illustrates that management of diabetes may not be easy. It requires careful thought, record keeping, discipline with the ketogenic diet, and frequent blood-glucose and ketone monitoring. The good news is all of this can result in improved glycemic control and a reduction in hypoglycemic and hyperglycemic episodes. Jack can be certain that if he continues to carefully manage his diabetes, he will likely be free of long-term complications and escape the shortened lifespan typical of many people with diabetes.

10

Hypoglycemic Drugs for T1DM

Let's now review oral and subcutaneously injected medications used for glycemic control in T1DM. When a properly formulated ketogenic diet, insulin therapy, and regular exercise are not enough to improve glycemic control, then one or more non-insulin medications can be added.

Every drug used to treat a medical condition has potential adverse effects. These effects range from minor symptoms to major life-threatening and fatal reactions. Therefore, using all available information, a judgment must be made concerning the risk-to-benefit ratio. Doctors prescribing medication try to minimize this ratio. Largely, this is an assessment of whether the benefits of a medication outweigh its potential risks. You can appreciate how difficult it is to predict this for a specific individual.

With the widely available Internet, every patient and physician has access to information about medication benefits, risks, and side effects on websites that include rxlist.com, drugs.com, and many others. We will be discussing benefits and risks of three classes of hypoglycemic medications that apply to T1DM in the following sections. There is extensive information about these medications, but we certainly cannot cover it all, so we will focus on the more important points. Our goal in this chapter is to give you a "pros and cons" overview of the available hypoglycemic medications so that you can make an informed choice if your physician suggests that you begin taking any of them.

Metformin

Metformin is effective in treating insulin resistance with a low side-effect profile. It was first introduced to the United Kingdom in 1958, Canada in 1972, and the United States in 1995, and it is now believed to be the most widely prescribed antidiabetic drug in the world.

Metformin is occasionally used "off-label" in conjunction with insulin in T1DM to address insulin resistance resulting from weight gain and the high doses of insulin needed to treat a high-carbohydrate diet. "Off-label" means that the FDA has not approved the use of the drug for a particular disease or condition, usually because the manufacturer has not funded, conducted, and submitted the results of research studies to the FDA. "Off-label" does not necessarily mean that use of that drug for that condition is not a good idea.

Although a switch to a ketogenic diet may be all that is necessary to resolve insulin resistance, overweight/obesity, and poor glycemic control, metformin may be appropriate during the transition or if there is difficulty being strict with the ketogenic diet.

Metformin lowers blood glucose by decreasing liver-glucose production and improves insulin sensitivity by increasing cellular-glucose uptake and utilization. It has the following clinical advantages:

- Extensive experience with the medication
- No association with weight gain
- Low cost

The disadvantages of adding Metformin to insulin include a possible increase in the likelihood of hypoglycemia, especially if the insulin dose is not appropriately reduced in response to switching to a ketogenic diet or adding metformin to an insulin regimen. In addition, a Vitamin B12 deficiency can occur in 7% of those taking metformin as a long-term therapy, and there is a very small risk for lactic acidosis, especially if there are underlying health factors such as heart failure or hypoxia.[92]

Metformin can also deplete vitamin B9 (folic acid). Gastrointestinal symptoms including nausea, diarrhea, and abdominal cramping.

Starting at a low dose and increasing the dose slowly can minimize these GI side effects.

In a study titled "The benefits of metformin therapy during continuous subcutaneous insulin infusion treatment of type 1 diabetic patients," the T1DM patients given metformin in the study showed that significant reductions of total cholesterol and LDL cholesterol were observed in patients treated with metformin. Treatment with metformin was associated with a reduction in daily insulin requirements after twenty-four weeks of -4.3 ± 9.9 units compared with an increase with placebo treatment of 1.7 ± 8.3 units, but no improvement in HbA1c. The number of hypoglycemic events (<60 mg/dL) with or without clinical symptoms during twenty-four weeks in the metformin group compared with the placebo group was 47.2 ± 26.8 vs. 45.1 ± 23.5 events, respectively. The metformin group did have a greater number of severe hypoglycemic episodes, nineteen in the metformin group, compared to eight in the placebo group.[93]

A 2010 systematic review by Vella et al. and published in Diabetologia considered all published studies on the use of metformin in T1DM and concluded that "Metformin reduces insulin-dose requirement in type 1 diabetes but it is unclear whether this is sustained beyond one year and whether there are benefits for cardiovascular and other key clinical outcomes."[94]

Glucagon-Like Peptide-1 (GLP-1) Agonists

GLP-1 agonists are used primarily in persons with T2DM. Only recently have clinical trials been initiated to test their effects in T1DM. Their use is currently off-label, as the manufacturer and the FDA have not approved their use for T1DM.

In type 2 diabetics with a functioning pancreas, GLP-1 stimulates insulin secretion while suppressing glucagon secretion. Such glucose-dependent action is particularly attractive because when plasma glucose is in the normal fasting range, GLP-1 no longer stimulates insulin that might lead to hypoglycemia. GLP-1 also appears to restore glucose sensitivity of pancreatic beta cells. GLP-1 is also known to inhibit pancreatic beta-cell apoptosis (programmed cell death) and stimulate the proliferation and differentiation of insulin-secreting beta cells. In addition, GLP-1 inhibits gastric secretion and motility, which delay nutrient absorption and lead to less hunger. However, once in circulation, GLP-1 is quickly degraded by the enzyme dipeptidyl peptidase-4 (DPP-4).

For type 1 diabetics, the drug allows for better glycemic control. Liraglutide (Victoza) is a GLP-1 agonist with a 97% amino acid sequence identity to natural human GLP-1. Unlike native GLP-1, liraglutide is stable against metabolic degradation by both DPP-4 and neutral endopeptidases, and can stay in the bloodstream for thirteen hours after subcutaneous administration, which allows for once daily dosing. Consider a paper published by Harrison et al. in the *Journal of Investigative Medicine*. The authors did a retrospective chart audit of patients with T1DM managed with an insulin pump who were prescribed the GLP-1 analog, liraglutide (Victoza). Patients who had at least one follow-up appointment after twenty weeks were noted to have a significant decrease in weight (4.2% from baseline) and a reduction in A1C from 7.4% to 7.0%. The total daily dose of insulin decreased 19.2%. There was no increase in hypoglycemia. Thus, patients with T1DM were able to improve their glycemic control on less exogenous insulin without experiencing an increase in hypoglycemia and were able to lose weight when liraglutide was added to insulin-pump therapy. The only notable side effect was nausea, which improved with time and/or dose reduction in this short-term chart review.[95]

Amylin Mimetic

Currently, the only available amylin mimetic is SYMLIN (pramlintide acetate) an injectable antihyperglycemic drug for use in individuals with T1DM or T2DM treated with insulin. Pramlintide is a synthetic analog of human amylin. Amylin is a naturally occurring neuroendocrine hormone produced by beta cells in the pancreas that contributes to glucose control after meals. It works by three different mechanisms, only one of which is helpful to those following a ketogenic diet. First, amylin, as well as pramlintide, suppresses glucagon secretion by the pancreatic alpha cells. This helps lower blood glucose and HbA1c, however, it lowers glucose in a glucose-independent fashion and, therefore, can cause hypoglycemia. The other two mechanisms of action include slowing of carbohydrate absorption and suppressing appetite, both of which are afforded by a ketogenic diet.

In a meta-analysis of three studies done by Lee et al. and published in the Annals of Family Medicine, pramlintide (Symlin) was somewhat more effective than the placebo in T1DM patients using conventional insulin therapy, with a between-group difference in HbA1c levels of 0.2% to 0.3% (two studies), but it was no more effective than the placebo in one study. Pramlintide-treated patients with both T1DM and T2DM experienced more weight loss compared with placebo-treated patients who tended to gain weight. Patients treated with pramlintide experienced more frequent nausea and severe hypoglycemia compared with patients treated with the placebo.[96] The cost is high compared with metformin and would not be expected to add much benefit to the combination of a ketogenic diet, exercise, and insulin.

Sodium-Glucose Cotransporter 2 (SGLT2) Inhibitors

SGLT2 inhibitors are the newest class of hypoglycemic agents for T2DM. However, some physicians are prescribing this medication to persons with T1DM who have poor glycemic control. The following is provided to caution readers about using this class of medications for T1DM. Canagliflozin was approved by the FDA in 2013 and dapagliflozin in 2014. Ipragliflozin is the first SGLT2 inhibitor approved in Japan. Empagliflozin has recently been approved in Europe and the United States. These medications block the kidneys' ability to reabsorb filtered glucose resulting in glucose appearing in the urine (glycosuria), a situation that usually only occurs in persons with uncontrolled diabetes. Full-dose SGLT2 inhibition induces a rapid increase in urinary glucose excretion, ranging from 50 to 100 g/day equally in men and women and lasting slightly longer than twenty-four hours. When on a ketogenic diet, this meets or exceeds the total daily carbohydrate intake. Any glucose excreted in excess of the daily carbohydrate intake must come from liver glycogenolysis and gluconeogenesis. This could place an unnecessary demand on the liver to produce glucose. Side effects include urinary tract infections, osmotic diuresis (similar effect to a diuretic), genital mycotic infections, euglycemic and hyperglycemic diabetic ketoacidosis, and hyperkalemia (high blood potassium), especially in persons with impaired kidney function.

In addition, concern has risen regarding the use of SGLT2 inhibitors in T1DM that they may increase the risk of euglycemic (blood glucose not particularly elevated) diabetic ketoacidosis.[97] The fact that the blood glucose is not unusually elevated would tend to make both patients and their doctors not suspect the diagnosis of DKA. Correspondence published in the Lancet included the following concern:

> Investigators of at least one study have reported an increased incidence of ketonuria among patients with type 1 diabetes treated with an SGLT inhibitor. Additionally, SGLT inhibition has been associated with increased glucagon concentration in patients with type 2 diabetes. Although insulinopenia is implicated indirectly in ketogenesis, glucagon is implicated directly and is potently lipolytic and ketogenic.

It is theoretically possible that a ketogenic diet could further increase the likelihood of that occurring, especially in those who require insulin therapy. For this reason, in our opinion, SGLT2 inhibitors should be used with extra caution or avoided altogether on a ketogenic diet.

A Note on Nutritional Supplements

Various natural supplements can have an effect on blood-sugar levels, especially when combined or used with the drugs discussed above.

In particular, caution should be exercised when combining insulin therapy with the following supplements:

- Alpha Lipoic Acid
- Bilberry
- Berberine
- Chromium
- Cinnamon
- Garlic
- Gingko Biloba
- Ginseng
- Green Tea Catechins
- Melatonin
- Resveratrol
- St. John's Wort
- Vanadium

Taking these supplements while using insulin can increase the risk of low blood sugar, especially when multiple supplements are taken.

Part 4

Exercise and Other Factors

11

The Role of Exercise

Although the body of research on exercise in relation to T1DM is not robust, we believe exercise plays an important role in health maintenance.[98] However, before starting any exercise program, consult with your physician. If you have coronary artery disease, known or unknown, starting an exercise program can precipitate a coronary event such as heart attack or arrhythmia.

Once you have your doctor's clearance, an exercise program that gradually progresses in duration and intensity will be beneficial in the longer term. Even if you haven't exercised on a regular basis for years, it's not too late to start.

Exercise can improve many health markers, and it increases muscle insulin sensitivity, which translates to lower insulin doses. Even for those who are sedentary, a single exercise session can improve glucose uptake in muscle. After a single session of moderate-intensity exercise, glucose uptake can increase by at least 40%. According to various studies, improvement in insulin sensitivity diminishes within sixteen to seventy-two hours after the last exercise session, so regular exercise is needed to maintain improved insulin sensitivity. Regular exercise also results in the development of other highly beneficial physical changes:

- Stronger bones, muscles, and tendons
- Stronger heart and lungs[99]
- Improved balance and resistance to falls
- Improved mental health

For those with T1DM, exercise definitely affects blood-sugar control, and we need to know how to handle it. Intense resistance (lifting heavy weights) or aerobic exercise (sprinting) increases the secretion of epinephrine (the fight-or-flight hormone, also called adrenaline), which can result in an increase in blood sugar. In non-diabetics, this process is regulated by insulin release from the pancreas so that blood glucose remains close to normal during exercise. In people with T1DM, this regulatory capability is lost or deficient, such that normal glucose release into the blood stream is unopposed, which results in hyperglycemia. The combination of increased insulin sensitivity and higher blood glucose after exercise will most likely change your insulin needs once you start an exercise program. In contrast, prolonged moderate aerobic exercise often results in increased muscle glucose uptake, and when basal insulin continues to be released from its injection site, it can lead to hypoglycemia. This is one advantage of an insulin pump. Pump users can decrease the basal insulin rate prior to or at the start of aerobic exercise and possibility avert hypoglycemia.

Unfortunately, the exact glycemic response to exercise is quite variable from one person to the next and even from one day to the next. Thus, one must be prepared to deal with either an increase or decrease in blood sugar during and after exercise by monitoring blood glucose frequently and taking a small insulin correction dose or glucose tablet(s) or liquid as needed.

Regular aerobic exercise like brisk walking is valuable, but just adding extra activity while going through your daily routine can be beneficial as well. For instance, the following activities are easy to incorporate into your day and, over time, can make a significant difference in the management of insulin sensitivity and achieving better blood-glucose levels.

- Walk to nearby destinations instead of driving
- Get off the bus a stop early and walk the rest of the way
- Work in the garden, rake leaves, or wash the car
- Play actively with kids or pets

- Walk around while talking on the phone
- Park at the far end of store parking lots and walk
- Avoid elevators and escalators, and choose to take the stairs as often as possible.

Carb-Adapted versus Keto-Adapted Muscles

Many people wonder how to fuel themselves with carbohydrates or other nutrients before, during, and after athletic training and events. We believe the strategy should be different from the "carbohydrate loading" advice usually given.

For the past sixty years or so, athletes have been taught that muscles perform best with carbohydrates. Fat-adaptation has not been on their radar at all. These athletes have been taught to eat carbohydrates before, during, and after exercise. Eating carbohydrates just before exercise increases glycogen stores in both muscle and liver. Those carbohydrates also increase insulin secretion, which inhibits fat oxidation and ketone production.

Chronic carbohydrate ingestion also results in muscles that are carb-adapted and, therefore, dependent upon glucose and glycogen as energy sources. The majority of athletes are carb-adapted, so they must consume some form of carbohydrate to supply glucose their muscles require, especially during prolonged aerobic exercise. While this may not be a problem for young, lean, insulin sensitive athletes, many others may store and retain excess fat or develop metabolic syndrome or diabetes as they get older, despite their exercise.

Athletes with a carbohydrate-fueling strategy can also run out of glycogen stores and "bonk" or "hit the wall." Because the carb-adapted athlete does not have the metabolic flexibility to burn fat at a sufficient rate, nor the ability to ingest enough carbohydrate to match energy expenditure, the supply of energy eventually fails to sustain athletic performance.

Dr. Jeff Volek showed that athletes who had been fat- and keto-adapted by following a low carbohydrate diet (LC) for months were able to utilize fat at a rate 2.3 times that of high carb-adapted (HC) athletes. A new finding was that LC athletes had equal levels of muscle glycogen pre-exercise, immediately post-exercise, and 2 hours post-exercise as the HC athletes. Thus, moderate intensity exercise can certainly be fueled with a low carbohydrate diet. Although not formally studied in patients with diabetes, improved fat and ketone utilization by muscle during exercise certainly has potential advantages for those with diabetes including less risk of hypoglycemia particularly for those who require insulin, meglitinide, or sulfonylurea medications for diabetes.[100]

The diabetic athlete who tries to mimic carbohydrate ingestion during exercise, with the goal of fueling muscle or simply to prevent hypoglycemia, may develop hyperglycemia due to the flood of stress hormones associated with exercise and carbohydrate ingestion without compensatory insulin secretion. In contrast, when carb intake is restricted, especially to a ketogenic level, the equilibrium shifts in the opposite direction. The keto-adapted diabetic athlete, by being able to utilize muscle triglyceride stores, may have a reduced need for both glucose and insulin. The liver, especially on a ketogenic diet, makes ketones during prolonged exercise, and this utilization of both fat and ketones may result in fewer episodes of hypoglycemia.

The potential for hyperglycemia due to stress hormone release during exercise still exists. Should hyperglycemia occur during or after exercise, insulin can be used to correct it, but it should be used with caution: exercise also improves insulin sensitivity and makes any dose more potent in lowering blood glucose. Remember to start with small doses at first.

Exercise also leads to improvements in well-being as shown in many health markers, and so we encourage all those with diabetes to make the effort to incorporate a regular enjoyable exercise routine into their lifestyle after they have been screened by their physician to participate.

Benefits of a Ketogenic Diet for Diabetic Athletes

Becoming fat-adapted and keto-adapted can provide the diabetic athlete with several advantages. Being keto-adapted means that enzymes and transport proteins needed in every step of fat and ketone production and utilization are enhanced. Thus, the following factors are increased:

- Access to fat stores
- Ability to make ketones
- Ability to oxidize fatty acids and ketones for energy

Similarly, the body no longer needs as much muscle glycogen, which can decrease by as much as 50% in the fat-adapted athlete.[101] However, a more recent study of fat-adapted athletes by Jeff Volek showed that muscle glycogen stores were not depleted and that less glycogen and more than twice as much fat was oxidized (burned) for muscle energy.[100] Thus, becoming fat-adapted means that muscles burn fatty acids and ketones preferentially and are less dependent on glucose.

In summary, becoming keto-adapted provides potential benefits to the diabetic athlete, including a reduction in hypoglycemia, hyperglycemia, and fuel exhaustion, and improved fuel flow and energy utilization from readily accessible fat stores. Since there are factors that tend to both increase and decrease blood glucose during exercise, the blood-glucose response to exercise is not necessarily predictable. Therefore, be prepared to test blood glucose and treat if needed with glucose tablets or liquid before, during, and after exercise. For those taking insulin, decreasing the dose of basal and/or rapid-acting insulin before exercise may also help prevent hypoglycemia.

Keto-Adaptation for Non-Diabetic Athletes

Are there advantages to becoming fat-adapted and keto-adapted for non-diabetic athletes? The possibility does indeed exist, and there are elite ultramarathon athletes winning and setting course records while on a low-carbohydrate diet. For example, Timothy Olsen is a low-carb athlete and is the current record holder of the 100-mile Western States Ultramarathon with a time of 14:46:44.[102] Zach Bitter, another low-carb athlete, has set several ultramarathon records, including the current 100-Mile American Record with a time of 11:47:21.[103]

12

Other Factors to Consider

The following information is offered in answer to common questions about the ketogenic diet, including vegetarianism, illness, stress, exercise and other issues.

Ketogenic Diet and Vegetarianism

Recommendations for treating diabetes with a ketogenic diet call for a carbohydrate intake of less than 50 grams per day with the goal of reducing blood-sugar levels and insulin needs. For most people, eating a moderate amount of protein and staying below an intake of 50 grams of carbohydrate per day results in ketosis.

Adhering to a vegetarian diet that restricts animal fats and proteins necessarily requires eating more carbohydrate. This higher carbohydrate intake can have the effect of increasing baseline blood sugar and short-circuiting ketosis. It is possible to eat a lower carb vegetarian diet. A book called the *New Atkins for a New You: The Ultimate Diet for Shedding Weight and Feeling Great* by Dr. Eric Westman, Dr. Jeff Volek, and Dr. Stephen Phinney is recommended, as it has a vegetarian section, as does the Atkins website.

As stated on the Atkins website, the recommendations for carbohydrate intake for vegetarians start at 30 carbohydrates per day, which is right in line with a ketogenic diet for diabetes. For those who follow a variation of a vegetarian diet, eggs, dairy, and fish are excellent sources of protein, fat, and many micronutrients. A vegan diet which excludes all animal products is more challenging because legumes and soya become major sources of protein. These protein sources also contain significant amounts of carbohydrate that can prevent ketosis. Nevertheless, a carbohydrate-restricted vegan diet would be more beneficial than the standard American diet for those with diabetes. There are some resources on the web that might help with a vegetarian or vegan low-carb diet. A Google search with the terms vegan or vegetarian and low carb should provide a few choices.

How Long Should I Stay on the Diet?

A change to better eating habits should be permanent so that the resulting benefits are also permanent. Going back to your old high-carb eating habits will only result in a loss of blood-sugar control, in blood-sugar elevations, and in diabetic complications; you'll be right back where you started. Think of this diet as a new way of eating that helps you regain your health and your life, rather than a temporary diet.

Alcohol Consumption While on the Diet

Straight spirits and dry red wines are optional while on a ketogenic diet. Please be aware that when one is in ketosis, the consumption of alcohol can have a greater, faster effect on your mental and physical condition. Moderation and self-experimentation are essential. Individuals will need to go slowly and monitor and assess the effects of alcohol on their blood glucose and ketone levels, adjusting intake as effects are noted.

Be aware that alcohol has no nutrients and is a toxic substance that must be metabolized through the liver to detoxify and excrete it. When consumed in significant amounts (more than one drink per day), alcohol has adverse effects on the liver, and this is especially true for those with diabetes. This is in addition to the widely known adverse effects of alcohol on brain function and behavior. In addition, alcohol can result in worsening blood-sugar control, including hyperglycemia and hypoglycemia in persons with diabetes. Hypoglycemia can be precipitated by alcohol consumption without food. Heavy alcohol consumption without food can also cause alcoholic ketoacidosis.

Alcohol can, by itself, cause many of the same complications as diabetes and, of course, add to the risk of developing them in those with diabetes. Such complications include nerve damage, eye damage, heart disease, and high blood pressure.

A paper aptly titled Consequences of Alcohol Use in Diabetics provides additional details on the effects of alcohol ingestion in persons with diabetes.[104] There are no significant health benefits from drinking alcohol, despite reports about the "antioxidant" polyphenols like resveratrol in red wine. Beers contain other nonalcoholic carbohydrates as they are made from grain, and mixed drinks often contain sugar.

This is the bottom line: It is Dr. Runyan's opinion that the adverse effects of alcohol in persons with diabetes far exceed any potential health benefits; therefore, alcohol consumption is not recommended. Should one decide to drink alcohol, it should be no more than one drink on an occasional basis and should be taken with food, especially if you are following a ketogenic diet.

How Stress Affects Ketosis

Stress can be a confounding factor for achieving your target blood-glucose levels because it affects hormones, which can increase blood glucose. When we are "stressed out" the body releases many types of flight-or-fight hormones, which drive up blood glucose and result in the need for more insulin. While it is unrealistic to expect to avoid stress, it's a good idea to minimize external causes of stress and find some relaxation techniques to help reduce it. Yoga, meditation, craftwork, listening to music, and gardening are all good forms of relaxation techniques.

Ketone Supplementation

Ketone supplements are becoming more popular, and we are often asked about the use of these products. Although there is some research evidence that they are beneficial in the athletic performance world, as of 2017, no studies have been published which looked at the effects of these products for those with diabetes.

Some people have asked about using them during the transition period of adopting a ketogenic diet to minimize hypoglycemia. Theoretically, it is possible that ketone supplements could be used to guard against the symptoms of hypoglycemia, but this use has not been tested in controlled studies, so we have no data to say that it is valid. In addition, the effects of ketone supplementation only last a few hours, so they would need to be taken quite often to work. Since these products are expensive, the cost of this solution reduces its usefulness.

Ketone supplements elevate blood beta-hydroxybutyrate temporarily, but are a source of extra calories without any other nutrients. In persons without diabetes, exogenous ketones also lower blood glucose. Since they have not been tested in persons with diabetes, it is not possible to predict their effect on blood glucose. Hence, use of these products would need to be taken into account in relation to diabetic medications and insulin dosing, so that blood sugar is not inadvertently reduced to dangerous levels.

Skeptical Physicians and Diabetes Educators

If your physician or diabetes educator is skeptical about the efficacy of ketogenic diets for the treatment of diabetes, please give him or her a copy of a published review article titled "Dietary carbohydrate restriction as the first approach in diabetes management." It presents a 12-point list of reasons supporting why ketogenic diets are the logical treatment of choice, and it refutes common misconceptions with strong science. The burden of proof is on the skeptic once this paper is read and understood.[10]

Resources for More Information

The following websites, videos and books are recommended as resources for obtaining more information about ketogenic diets and/or diabetes.

Website Resources

- Ellen's website: ketogenic-diet-resource.com
- Dr. Runyan's website: ketogenicdiabeticathlete.wordpress.com
- Dr. Richard Bernstein's website: www.diabetes-book.com
- Jeff Volek's YouTube talk on "The Many Facets of Keto-Adaptation": www.youtube.com/watch?v=GC1vMBRFiwE
- Kelley Pounds' Low Carb RN website: www.lowcarbrn.com
- Dr. Andreas Eenfeldt's website Diet Doctor: www.dietdoctor.com/diabetes
- Dr. Jay Wortman's *My Big Fat Diet* documentary on treating diabetes in a First Nation community: www.mybigfatdiet.net
- Jenny Ruhl's Diabetes 101 website: www.phlaunt.com
- David Mendosa's diabetes website: www.mendosa.com
- D-Solve diabetes website: dsolve.com
- Type One Grit Facebook group: https://www.facebook.com/groups/660633730675058/

Recommended Books

- *Dr. Bernstein's Diabetes Solution* by Richard K. Bernstein, MD
- *The Diabetes Diet: Dr. Bernstein's Low-Carbohydrate Solution* by Richard K. Bernstein, MD
- *The Art and Science of Low Carbohydrate Living: An Expert's Guide to Making the Life-Saving Benefits of Carbohydrate Restriction Sustainable and Enjoyable* by Jeff Volek and Stephen Phinney

- *The Art and Science of Low Carbohydrate Performance* by Jeff Volek, PhD, RD, and Stephen Phinney, MD, PhD

- *Good Calories, Bad Calories* by Gary Taubes

- *Why We Get Fat: And What to Do About It* by Gary Taubes

- *Ketogenic Diets: Treatments for Epilepsy and Other Disorders, Fifth Edition* by John M. Freeman, MD, Eric Kossoff, MD, Zahava Turner, RD and James E. Rubenstein, MD

- *Living Low Carb: Controlled-Carbohydrate Eating for Long-Term Weight Loss* by Jonny Bowden, PhD, CNS, and Barry Sears, PhD

- *The Low Carb Dietitian's Guide to Health and Beauty: How a Whole-Foods, Low-Carbohydrate Lifestyle Can Help You Look and Feel Better Than Ever* by Franziska Spritzler and Jacqueline A. Eberstein

- *Dr. Atkins' New Diet Revolution* by Robert C. Atkins, MD

- *New Atkins for a New You: The Ultimate Diet for Shedding Weight and Feeling Great* by Eric Westman, MD; Jeff Volek, PhD, RD; and Stephen Phinney, MD, PhD

- *Keto Clarity: Your Definitive Guide to the Benefits of a Low-Carb, High-Fat Diet* by Jimmy Moore and Eric Westman MD

- *The New Atkins Made Easy: A Faster, Simpler Way to Shed Weight and Feel Great—Starting Today!* by Colette Heimowitz

- *The Big Fat Surprise: Why Butter, Meat and Cheese Belong in a Healthy Diet* by Nina Teicholz

- *The Case Against Sugar* by Gary Taubes

Appendixes

Appendix A
Supplement Recommendations

Micronutrients are just as important as macronutrients. Micronutrients include vitamins, antioxidants, electrolytes, and minerals, and they are required in small quantities to support a range of physiological functions. These can be obtained from meat, organ meat, bone broth, fish, eggs, nuts, seeds, animal fats, tropical oils, non-starchy vegetables, and low-sugar fruits—all of which make up a ketogenic diet.

Although a balanced diet of real foods can provide many of the micronutrients needed, supplements can be helpful. Look for those with the lowest carbohydrate levels. Read labels to rule out those that contain sugar alcohols or other hidden carbohydrates. The following supplements are recommended:

- A carbohydrate-free multivitamin/mineral supplement. Make sure it contains at least 100% of the RDA for selenium and zinc. The Nature's Life Mighty Mini Vite Micro Tablet product offers just the minimal baseline coverage and is recommended.
- Vitamin D3 in the form of cholecalciferol, 2000 IU. The Country Life brand offers a gel-cap product with medium-chain triglycerides.
- Magnesium citrate, 400 mg daily, taken at bedtime if possible. You can also use a product called Natural Calm. It's a powder that can be mixed into a beverage and sipped throughout the day.
- CoQ10 (Ubiquinol or Ubiquinone), 100 mg daily.
- Now brand potassium chloride powder. It is very important to get enough potassium each day. Drinking homemade mineral water is one option, as is including green vegetables, small amounts of nuts, and plenty of avocadoes in your diet on a regular basis.
- CardiaSalt, Lite Salt, or NuSalt. You can find these salt substitutes at most grocery stores or on Amazon. You can use regular salt or these salt substitutes for flavoring your food.

- Homemade mineral water: Follow the recipe below EXACTLY, and sip this water only if you have symptoms such as fatigue, dizziness or headaches. (See Possible Side Effect 3 in chapter 3.)

Homemade Mineral Water

To 1 quart of cold water add exactly 1/4 teaspoon of Now brand potassium chloride powder AND exactly 1 level teaspoon of table or sea salt (provides sodium and chloride). Mix well and store in the refrigerator.

If you prefer not to take supplements, we have created a list of various nutrient-dense foods and the micronutrient amounts that each contains. You can download a document containing the Food Nutrient Lists from the bottom of the "About this Site/Resources" page on the ketogenic-diet-resource.com website.

Appendix B

Suggested Daily Protein Amounts

These tables provide baseline minimum and maximum protein gram needs for most people based on the goal body weight.

Goal weight (lb.)	Goal weight (kg)	Minimum protein grams per day (1.0g/kg)	Maximum protein grams per day (1.5g/kg)
110	50	50	75
115	52	52	78
120	54	54	82
125	57	57	85
130	59	59	88
135	61	61	92
140	64	64	95
145	66	66	99
150	68	68	102
155	70	70	105
160	73	73	109
165	75	75	112
170	77	77	116
175	79	79	119
180	82	82	122
185	84	84	126
190	86	86	129
195	88	88	133
200	91	91	136
205	93	93	139
210	95	95	143
215	98	98	146
220	100	100	150
225	102	102	153
230	104	104	156
235	107	107	160
240	109	109	163
245	111	111	167
250	113	113	170
255	116	116	174
260	118	118	177
265	120	120	180
270	122	122	184
275	125	125	187
280	127	127	191
285	129	129	194
290	132	132	197

Appendix C
Food Reference Lists

The food lists in this appendix are by no means comprehensive, but they should address most of the common foods suitable for a ketogenic diet. There are many online resources available, which contain thousands of food listings. We've recommended several in this book:

- Cronometer.com has a ketogenic option.
- Fitday.com offers both a web-based application and an application that can be downloaded to a PC.
- Myfitnesspal.com offers both a web-based and mobile application, and is another good choice, and it's free.
- The USDA's free nutrition database (http://ndb.nal.usda.gov).
- Atkins.com also has some tools for tracking progress on a ketogenic diet plan.

There are many food-count books on the market too:

- *The Calorie King* book gets good reviews on Amazon, and it comes in both a paperback and digital edition.
- *The Complete Book of Food Counts,* ninth edition, by Corrine Netzer.
- *Dana Carpender's Carb and Calorie Counter.*

The food lists begin on the next page.

Fat and Oil Foods

	Calories	Fat (g)	Carbs (g)	Fiber (g)	Protein (g)
Avocado oil, 1 tbsp.	124	14	0	0	0
Avocado, Haas, 3 oz.	102	9	7	5	2
Bacon fat, 1 tbsp.	116	13	0	0	0
Beef tallow, 1 tbsp.	115	13	0	0	0
Butter, 1 tbsp.	102	12	0	0	0
Chicken fat, 1 tbsp.	115	13	0	0	0
Cocoa butter, 1 tbsp.	120	14	0	0	0
Coconut oil, 1 tbsp.	117	14	0	0	0
Cream cheese (block), 2 tbsp.	101	10	1	0	2
Flaxseed oil, 1 tbsp.	120	14	0	0	0
Ghee, 1 tbsp.	112	13	0	0	0
Heavy cream, fluid, 2 tbsp.	103	11	1	0	1
Lard, fresh (non-hydrogenated), 1 tbsp.	115	13	0	0	0
Macadamia oil, 1 tbsp.	120	14	0	0	0
Mayonnaise (full-fat), 1 tbsp.	99	11	1	0	0
MCT oil, 1 tbsp.	100	14	0	0	0
Olive oil, 1 tbsp.	119	14	0	0	0
Red palm oil, 1 tbsp.	120	14	0	0	0
Salad dressing, creamy, full-fat (<2 carb/serving), 1.5 tbsp.	130	14	1	0	1
Sour cream (full-fat, no fillers, e.g., Daisy brand), 4 tbsp.	120	10	2	0	2

High-Fat, Moderate-Protein Combination Foods

	Calories	Fat (g)	Carbs (g)	Fiber (g)	Protein (g)
Almond meal (flour), 1 oz.	160	14	6	3	6
Cheese, feta, 3 oz.	120	11	3	1	6
Coconut butter, 2 tbsp.	186	18	8	4	2
Coconut, dried, unsweetened, 1 oz.	165	15	6	4	3

Nuts, almond, roasted, 1 oz.	172	16	5	3	6
Nuts, Brazil, roasted, 1 oz.	186	19	3	2	4
Nuts, cashew, 1 oz.	164	14	10	0	8
Nuts, hazelnut, 1 oz.	183	18	5	3	4
Nuts, macadamia, roasted, 1 oz.	203	22	4	3	2
Nuts, pecan, roasted, 1 oz.	201	21	4	3	3
Nuts, walnut, 1 oz.	185	18	4	2	4
Seeds, chia, 1 oz.	140	10	12	10	4
Seeds, flax, 1 oz.	152	12	8	7	6
Seeds, pumpkin, roasted, 1 oz.	148	12	4	1	9
Seeds, sesame, 1 oz.	161	14	7	5	5
Seeds, sunflower, roasted, 1 oz.	168	15	6	3	6

High-Protein, Moderate-Fat Foods

	Calories	Fat (g)	Carbs (g)	Fiber (g)	Protein (g)
Bacon, cooked, 2 slices	92	9	2	0	4
Beef, ground, 80% lean, cooked, 1 oz.	74	5	0	0	7
Cheese, blue, 1 oz.	100	8	1	0	6
Cheese, brie, 1 oz.	95	8	0	0	6
Cheese, cheddar, natural, 1 oz.	114	9	0	0	7
Cheese, Mexican blend, 1 oz.	105	9	1	0	7
Cheese, Monterey Jack, 1 oz.	106	9	0	0	7
Cheese, mozzarella, part skim, 1 oz.	72	5	1	0	7
Cheese, mozzarella, whole milk, 1 oz.	90	7	1	0	6
Cheese, parmesan, hard, 1 oz.	111	7	1	0	10
Cheese, provolone, 1 oz.	100	8	1	0	7
Cheese, ricotta, whole milk, 0.25 cup	107	8	2	0	7
Cheese, Swiss, 1 oz.	108	8	2	0	8
Duck, roasted, skin eaten, 1 oz.	95	8	0	0	5
Egg, whole, large, plain, 1 ea.	72	5	0	0	6
Lamb, boneless, cooked, 1 oz.	83	6	0	0	7
Pork sausage, cooked, 1.5 oz.	102	9	0	0	7

Pork ribs, roasted, plain, 1 oz.	104	8	0	0	8
Pork shoulder, roasted, 1 oz.	82	6	0	0	7
Yogurt, Greek, full-fat, 3.5 oz.	95	5	4	0	9

Lean-Protein Foods

	Calories	Fat (g)	Carbs (g)	Fiber (g)	Protein (g)
Beef, ground, 92% lean, cooked, 1 oz.	45	2	0	0	7
Beef steak, broiled or baked, 1 oz.	71	4	0	0	8
Beef, chuck, blade roast, cooked, 1 oz.	75	4	0	0	9
Chicken breast, roasted or baked, skin not eaten, 1 oz.	46	1	0	0	9
Chicken thigh, roasted, no skin, 1.0 oz.	55	3	0	0	7
Clams, fresh, baked, 1 oz.	39	2	1	0	4
Cottage cheese, 1% or 2%, 0.25 cup	41	1	2	0	7
Crab, king, fresh, steamed, 1.5 oz.	41	0	0	0	7.5
Egg whites, raw, large egg, 2 ea.	34	0	0	0	7
Elk steak, roasted, 1 oz.	41	0.5	0	0	8.5
Fish fillet (flounder, sole, scrod), no breading, baked, 2 oz.	49	1	0	0	8.5
Fish, salmon fresh fillet, 1 oz.	39	1	0	0	7
Fish, salmon, canned, pink, 1 oz.	39	1	0	0	7
Ham, deli style, lean, 1 oz.	35	1	1	0	5
Ham, smoked, spiral, 1 oz.	53	3	1	0	5
Pork chops, lean, cooked, 1 oz.	57	3	0	0	7
Pork roast, loin, cooked, 1 oz.	70	4	0	0	8
Scallops, baked or broiled, 1 oz.	38	1	1	0	6
Shrimp, steamed or boiled, 1 oz.	39	1	0	0	8
Tuna, canned, water pack, 1 oz.	33	0	0	0	7
Turkey breast, roasted, no skin, 1 oz.	38	0	0	0	9
Turkey thigh, roasted, no skin, 1 oz.	52	2	0	0	8

Yogurt, Greek, 0% fat, 3 oz.	50	0	3.5	0	9

Carbohydrate Foods

	Calories	Fat (g)	Carbs (g)	Fiber (g)	Protein (g)
Asparagus, cooked, 1 cup	46	2	6	4	5
Beans, cooked (black, kidney) 0.25 cup	55	0	10	3	4
Beans, green, cooked, 1 cup	34	0.5	8	4	2
Blueberries, raw, whole, 0.25 cup	21	0	5	1	0
Broccoli, cooked, chopped, 0.5 cup	27	0	6	3	2
Brussels sprouts, raw, 1 cup	38	0	8	3	3
Cabbage, green, raw, shredded, 4 oz.	23	0	5	2	1
Carrots, baby, raw, 2 oz.	20	0	6	2	0
Cauliflower, cooked, 1 cup	28	0	6	2	2
Celery, raw, chopped, 1 cup	36	0	7	4	2
Chickpeas, cooked, ¼ cup	67	1	11	3	4
Cucumber, raw, sliced, 10 oz.	29	0	6	2	1
Eggplant, raw, 6 oz.	33	0	8	5	1
Garlic, 6 cloves	24	0	6	0	0
Green beans, cooked, 0.5 cup	22	0	5	1	1
Kale, raw, chopped, 2 oz.	28	0	6	1	2
Lemon juice, 1 tbsp.	3	0	1	0	0
Lettuce, any leaf, shredded, 3 cups	24	0	6	3	3
Lettuce, iceberg, shredded, 3 cups	24	0	6	3	0
Lettuce, romaine shredded, 3 cups	24	0	6	3	3
Lime juice, 1 tbsp.	3	0	1	0	0
Mushrooms, button, raw, 6 oz.	37	1	6	2	5
Mushrooms, portabella, raw, 4 oz.	29	0	6	2	3
Onion, green, 0.5 cup	16	0	4	1	1
Onion, white, raw, 0.5 cup	33	0	7	1	1
Pepper, bell, raw, 4 oz.	23	0	5	2	0
Potato, white, cooked, 0.5 cup	95	4	13	2	1

Raspberries, raw, whole, 0.5 cup	32	0	7	4	1
Rice, white, cooked, 0.25 cup	51	0	11	0	1
Shallots, chopped, 2 tbsp.	14	0	4	0	0
Spinach, cooked, from frozen, 5 oz.	57	3	5	3	4
Spinach, raw, 6 oz.	38	1	6	4	1
Squash, spaghetti, cooked, 1 cup	75	0	10	2	1
Squash, summer, cooked, sliced, 1 cup	36	0	8	3	2
Strawberries, raw, whole, 0.5 cup	23	0	6	2	0
Swiss chard, chopped coarse, 3 cups	21	0	4	2	2
Tomato sauce, 0.5 cup	40	0	8	2	2
Tomato, raw, 6 oz.	31	0	7	2	1
Turnips, raw, 4 oz.	32	0	7	2	1

Miscellaneous Foods

	Calories	Fat (g)	Carbs (g)	Fiber (g)	Protein (g)
Olives, black, 1 cup	141	13	8	4	1
Olives, green, 1 cup	193	20	5	4	1
Pork rinds, fried, 0.75 oz.*	116	7	0	0	13*

*Note on pork rinds: The protein in this food is inferior in quality. Count the protein grams but limit amounts eaten so as not to displace other more complete protein foods.

Spice Carb Counts

Spice	Carbs in 1 tbsp.
Allspice, ground	3.0
Basil, dried	0.9
Black pepper	2.4
Caraway seed	0.8
Cardamom, ground	2.4
Cayenne pepper	1.6
Cinnamon, ground	1.7
Cloves	1.7
Coriander seed	0.6
Cumin, ground	2.1
Curry powder	1.6
Fennel seed	0.7
Garlic powder	5.3
Ginger, ground	3.1
Imitation vanilla extract	0.3
Mace, ground	1.6
Nutmeg	2.0
Onion powder	5.2
Oregano, ground	0.4
Paprika	1.2
Parsley, dried	0.3
Peppermint, fresh	0.1
Poppy seeds	1.2
Poultry seasoning	2.0
Pumpkin-pie spice	3.1
Sage, ground	0.4
Spearmint, dried	0.3
Tarragon, ground	2.0
Thyme, ground	1.1
Vanilla extract	1.6
White pepper	3.0

Appendix D
Conversions and Measurements

Rules for Measures

- Multiply grams by 0.0353 to get the weight in ounces.
- Multiply ounces by 28.35 to get the weight in grams.

Dry Measure Equivalents

Measurement →	Equal to →	Equal to →	Equal to
3 teaspoons	1 tablespoon	1/2 ounce	14.3 grams
2 tablespoons	1/8 cup	1 ounce	28.3 grams
4 tablespoons	1/4 cup	2 ounces	56.7 grams
5 1/3 tablespoons	1/3 cup	2.6 ounces	75.6 grams
8 tablespoons	1/2 cup	4 ounces	113.4 grams
12 tablespoons	3/4 cup	6 ounces	169.8 grams
32 tablespoons	2 cups	16 ounces	452.8 grams

Volume (Liquid) Measurements

American cups and quarts equal to →	American ounces equal to →	Metric (milliliters and liters)
2 tbsp.	1 fl. oz.	30 ml
¼ cup	2 fl. oz.	60 ml
½ cup	4 fl. oz.	125 ml
1 cup	8 fl. oz.	250 ml
1 ½ cups	12 fl. oz.	375 ml
2 cups or 1 pint	16 fl. oz.	500 ml
4 cups or 1 quart	32 fl. oz.	1000 ml or 1 liter
1 gallon	128 fl. oz.	4 liters

Oven Temperatures

Fahrenheit	Celsius
250° F	130° C
300° F	150° C
350° F	180° C
400° F	200° C
450° F	230° C

Abbreviations

Abbrev.	Full term
ea.	each
oz.	ounce
tbsp.	tablespoon
tsp.	teaspoon

Ketone Conversion Formula

The exact calculation rule is shown here:

[Value in mg/dL] is divided by 10.41	mmol/L
[Value in mmol/L] multiplied by 10.41	mg/dL

The easier method:

[Value in mg/dL] divided by 10	mmol/L
[Value in mmol/L] multiplied by 10	mg/dL

Blood-Glucose Conversion Formula

The exact calculation rule shown below:

[Value in mg/dL] multiplied by 0.0555	mmol/L
[Value in mmol/L] multiplied by 18.0182	mg/dL

The easier method:

[Value in mg/dL] divided by 18	mmol/L
[Value in mmol/L] multiplied by 18	mg/dL

Blood-Glucose Conversion Table: mg/dL to mmol/L

mg/dL	mmol/L
50	3.0
55	3.1
60	3.3
65	3.6
70	3.9
75	4.2
80	4.4
85	4.7
90	5.0
95	5.3
100	5.6
105	5.8
110	6.1
115	6.4
120	6.7
125	6.9
130	7.2
135	7.5
140	7.8
145	8.1
150	8.3
155	8.6
160	8.9
165	9.2
170	9.4
175	9.7
180	10.0
185	10.3

Hemoglobin A1c (HbA1c) to Average Blood-Glucose Conversion

HbA1C	Average Blood Glucose	
	mg/dL	mmol/l
4.5	82	4.6
5	96	5.4
5.5	111	6.2
6	125	6.9
6.5	140	7.7
7	155	8.5
7.5	169	9.3
8	184	10.1
8.5	197	10.9
9	214	11.7
9.5	226	12.6
10	240	13.3
10.5	254	14.1
11	269	14.9
11.5	283	15.7
12	298	16.5
12.5	312	17.3
13	326	18.1
14	355	19.7
15	383	21.3
16	413	22.9
17	441	24.5

Appendix E
Legal Disclaimer and Terms of Use

This Legal Disclaimer and Terms of Use Agreement is entered into between Ellen Davis and Keith Runyan, MD, the authors of this document, the Ketogenic Diet Resource website and you. All of the information provided in and throughout this book (hereafter known as Publication) and offered at http://www.Keto-genic-Diet-Resource.com is intended solely for general information and should NOT be relied upon for any particular diagnosis, treatment, or care. This is not a substitute for medical advice or treatment. This Publication is only for general informational purposes. It is strongly encouraged that individuals and their families consult with qualified medical professionals for treatment and related advice on individual cases before beginning any diet. Decisions relating to the prevention, detection, and treatment of all health issues should be made only after discussing the risks and benefits with your health care provider, taking into account your personal medical history, your current situation, and your future health risks and concerns. If you are pregnant, nursing, diabetic, on medication, have a medical condition, or are beginning a health or weight-control program, consult your physician before using products or services discussed in this book and before making any other dietary changes. The authors and publisher cannot guarantee that the information in this Publication is safe and proper for every reader. For this reason, this Publication is sold without warranties or guarantees of any kind, express or implied, and the authors and publisher disclaim any liability, loss, or damage caused by the contents, either directly or consequentially. Neither the US Food and Drug Administration nor any other government regulatory body has evaluated statements made in this Publication. Products, services, and methods discussed in this Publication are not intended to diagnose, treat, cure, or prevent any disease.

Indemnification:

All users of this book agree to defend, indemnify, and hold harmless Ketogenic-Diet-Resource.com, its contributors, any entity jointly created by them, their respective affiliates and their respective directors, officers, employees, and agents from and against all claims and expenses, including attorneys' fees, arising out of the use of this Publication.

Disclaimer of Liability:

Neither Ketogenic-Diet-Resource.com nor its contributors shall be held liable for any use of the information described and/or contained herein and assumes no responsibility for anyone's use of the information. In no event shall the Ketogenic-Diet-Resource.com website or its contributors be liable for any direct, indirect, incidental, special, exemplary, or consequential damages (including but not limited to: procurement of substitute goods or services; loss of use, data, or profits; or business interruption) however caused and on any theory of liability, whether in contract, strict liability, tort (including negligence or otherwise), or any other theory arising in any way out of the use of this material, even if Ketogenic-Diet-Resource.com has been advised of the possibility of such damage. This disclaimer of liability applies to any damages or injury, whether based on alleged breach of contract, tortious behavior, negligence, or any other cause of action, including but not limited to damages or injuries caused by any failure of performance, error, omission, interruption, deletion, defect, delay in operation or transmission, computer virus, communication line failure, and/or theft, destruction, or unauthorized access to, alteration of, or use of any record.

Rules of Conduct: No Warranties:

All content in this Publication is provided to you on an "as is," "as available" basis without warranty of any kind, either express or implied, including but not limited to the implied warranties of merchantability, fitness for a particular purpose and non-infringement. Ketogenic-Diet-Resource.com makes no warranty as to the accuracy, completeness, currency, or reliability of any content available through this website. Ketogenic-Diet-Resource.com makes no representations or warranties of any kind that use of the website will be uninterrupted or error-free. The user is responsible for taking all precautions necessary to ensure that any web-based content offered from the website or Publication is free of viruses.

Limitation of Liability:

Ketogenic-Diet-Resource.com specifically disclaims any and all liability, whether based in contract, tort, strict liability or otherwise, for any direct, indirect, incidental, consequential, or special damages arising out of or in any way connected with access to or use of the website or Publication even if Ketogenic-Diet-Resource.com has been advised of the possibility of such damages. This limitation of liability includes, but is not limited to, reliance by any party on any content obtained through use of this website, or that arises in connection with mistakes or omissions in, or delays in transmission of information to or from the user, interruptions in telecommunications connections to this website, this Publication, or viruses, whether caused in whole or in part by negligence, acts of God, telecommunications failure, theft or destruction of or unauthorized access to the website, Publication, or related information.

Modifications:

Ketogenic-Diet-Resource.com reserves the right to modify this Publication and the rules and regulations governing its use at any time. Modifications will be posted on the website, and users are deemed to be apprised of and bound by any changes to the website. Your continued use of this Publication following the posting of changes to these Terms of Use constitutes your acceptance of those changes. Ketogenic-Diet-Resource.com may make changes in the products and/or services described in this Publication at any time.

Governing Law, Forum Selection, and General Provisions:

This Publication was created and uploaded by Ketogenic-Diet-Resource.com from its place of business in Wyoming, USA. Ketogenic-Diet-Resource.com makes no representation that the information in the Publication is appropriate or available for use in other locations. Access to the Publication from territories where the contents of the Publication may be illegal is prohibited. Those who choose to access this Publication from other locations do so at their own initiative and are responsible for compliance with applicable local laws. This Agreement shall be governed by and interpreted in accordance with the laws of Wyoming, USA., excluding the application of its conflicts of law rules, and all claims relating or arising out of this Agreement, whether sounding in contract, tort or otherwise, shall likewise be governed by the laws of Wyoming, USA, excluding the application of its conflicts of law rules. You agree that all actions or proceedings arising in connection with this Agreement shall be tried and litigated exclusively in the state and federal courts located in the County of Laramie, State of Wyoming, USA. The aforementioned choice of venue is intended to be mandatory and not permissive in nature, thereby precluding the possibility of litigation with respect to or arising out of this Agreement in any jurisdiction other than that specified in this paragraph. You agree that the state and federal courts located in the County of Laramie, State of Wyoming shall have in personam jurisdiction and venue over you for the purpose of litigating any dispute, controversy, or proceeding arising out of or related to this Agreement.

Severability

If a section of this disclaimer is determined by any court or other competent authority to be unlawful and/or unenforceable, the other sections of this disclaimer shall continue in effect.

References

Glossary

Acetoacetate (AcAc) A water soluble ketone body produced by the liver from the metabolism of fatty acids when carbohydrate intake is restricted and glycogen stores are low or the body is in a fasted state. It can be used as a fuel source by most normal cells in the body when blood-glucose availability is low. Acetoacetate can be converted into two other ketone bodies, beta-hydroxybutyrate and acetone. See also *ketone body, acetone* and *beta-hydroxybutyrate*.

Acetone One of the three types of ketone bodies, acetone is a spontaneous byproduct of the breakdown of acetoacetate. Acetone is expelled from the body via the breath.

Acidosis Acidosis is a condition in which the blood is too acidic (blood pH falls below 7.35), which manifests in the symptoms of rapid breathing, confusion, or lethargy. It can be fatal if not treated.

ADA American Diabetes Association

Adipose Fat tissue in the body.

Adiposity Measure of the amount of body fat.

Adrenalin See epinephrine. Also called the "fight or flight" response hormone.

Advanced glycation end-products (AGEs) Body proteins or fats that become glycated after exposure to sugars. AGEs are the common cause of diabetic complications. The presence and accumulation of AGEs in many different cell types affect extracellular and intracellular structure and function. Also see glycation.

Aerobic exercise Sustained cadenced exercise that increases your heart rate; also referred to as cardio.

AGEs See advanced glycation end-products and glycation.

Agonist A substance that acts like another substance and therefore stimulates an action.

Alpha cell Specialized cell in the pancreatic Islet of Langerhans that produces glucagon when the body needs it.

Amino acids The molecular building blocks of proteins. There are over three hundred different amino acids in nature. Humans depend on twenty different amino acids, and eight of those are essential—meaning they have to be obtained from the diet.

Amylin A hormone co-secreted with insulin by the beta cells of the pancreas that inhibits glucagon, delays emptying of the stomach, and acts to increase satiety.

Amyotrophic lateral sclerosis (ALS) A specific disorder that involves the death of neurons. ALS is characterized by stiff muscles, muscle twitching, and gradually worsening weakness due to muscle wasting. This results in difficulty speaking, swallowing, and eventually breathing.

Anoxic Total depletion in the level of oxygen.

Antioxidants Substances that neutralize harmful free radicals and reactive oxygen species.

Apoptosis   The metabolic process of programmed cell death. In normal cells, apoptosis is triggered when a cell is damaged to minimize toxic releases to surrounding cells. Cancer cells tend to have defective mechanisms to trigger apoptosis.

Arrhythmia   Any of a group of conditions in which the heartbeat is irregular or is faster or slower than normal.

Aspart (insulin)   Insulin aspart is a fast-acting insulin analog marketed by Novo Nordisk as NovoLog/NovoRapid. It is a manufactured form of human insulin where a single amino acid has been exchanged. This change helps the fast-acting insulin analog be absorbed quickly into the bloodstream.

Asymptomatic   Having no symptoms.

Atherosclerosis   Clogging, narrowing, and hardening of blood vessels by plaque deposits.

ATP   Adenosine triphosphate. A molecule that transports chemical energy within cells for metabolic purposes.

Basal insulin   The role of basal insulin, also known as background insulin, is to keep blood glucose at consistent levels during periods of fasting. Basal insulin has to act over a relatively long period of time; therefore, it will either be long-acting insulin or intermediate insulin.

Baseline blood sugar   The blood-sugar measurement before insulin or a meal is given.

Beta cells   Specialized cells in the pancreas that produce the hormones insulin and amylin.

Beta-hydroxybutyrate (BOHB)   A ketone body generated from the conversion of acetoacetate, the main ketone body produced by the liver from the metabolism of fatty acids when carbohydrate intake is restricted and glycogen stores are low or the body is in a fasted state. See also *acetone* and *acetoacetate*.

Blood glucose (sugar)   The amount of glucose or sugar in the bloodstream at any one time.

Blood lipids   The medical term for the total cholesterol, triglycerides, and HDL and LDL cholesterol in your blood.

Blood pressure   The pressure your blood exerts against the walls of your arteries during a heartbeat.

Body mass index (BMI)   A measure of body fat based on height and weight for adults.

Bolus insulin   A dose of insulin specifically taken at meal times to keep blood-glucose levels under control following a meal. Bolus insulin needs to act quickly, and so short-acting insulin or rapid-acting insulin will be used.

Carb-adaptation   The process of becoming adapted to using carbohydrates and glucose as the main cellular fuel.

Carbohydrate (carb)   Foods which are broken down by digestion into simple sugars such as glucose to provide a source of energy. Examples are starches, such as potatoes, wheat, rice and corn, and sweet foods, such as sugar, candy, cookies, and ice cream.

Cerebrovascular   Pertaining to the blood vessels and, especially, the arteries that supply the brain.

CGM Continuous glucose monitor. Also known as real-time continuous glucose monitor (rt-CGM). A device with a tiny glucose sensor that is inserted under the skin to measure glucose levels in tissue fluid after it has been calibrated initially and every twelve hours thereafter using a blood-glucose meter reading.

Cholesterol A waxy substance essential for many of the body's functions, including manufacturing hormones and making cell membranes.

Cortisol A steroid hormone that is produced by the adrenal glands. It is released in response to stress and a low level of blood glucose. Its functions are to increase blood sugar through gluconeogenesis, to suppress the immune system, and to aid the metabolism of fat, protein, and carbohydrate.

CSII A device that delivers a continuous subcutaneous insulin infusion, also known as an insulin pump.

CVD Cardiovascular disease, also known as "hardening of the arteries" or heart disease.

Dawn phenomenon Sometimes called the dawn effect, this is an early morning (usually between 2:00 am and 8:00 am) increase in blood sugar not associated with food intake. May be driven by a rise in a hormone called cortisol.

Diabetes See TD1M and T2DM or type 1 diabetes and type 2 diabetes.

Diabetic gastroparesis A disorder affecting people with type 1 and type 2 diabetes in which the stomach takes too long to empty its contents. It can make diabetes worse by making it more difficult to manage blood glucose.

Diabetic ketoacidosis (DKA) A life-threatening condition associated with insulin deficiency causing high blood sugar, dehydration, and an excess of ketone bodies, which render blood pH acidic. Treatment consists of emergency fluid and insulin treatment.

Diet-heart hypothesis The hypothesis that a high intake of saturated fat and elevated LDL cholesterol are the most important causes of atherosclerosis and coronary heart disease. Also known as the lipid-heart hypothesis.

Diuretic Any substance that causes fluid to be eliminated from the body by increasing urination.

Dyslipidemia An elevation of plasma cholesterol, triglycerides (TGs), or both, or a low high-density lipoprotein level that contributes to the development of atherosclerosis. Diagnosis is made by measuring plasma levels of total cholesterol, TGs, and individual lipoproteins.

Endogenous Sourced from within the body; having an internal cause or origin.

Epidemiological Sourced in epidemiology, the science that studies the patterns, causes, and effects of health and disease conditions in defined populations. It is the cornerstone of public health, and informs policy decisions and evidence-based practice by identifying risk factors for disease and targets for preventive health care.

Epinephrine More commonly known as adrenaline; a hormone secreted by the sympathetic nervous system and adrenal glands in response to low blood sugar when insufficient ketones are available. It causes an increase in blood glucose by the release of glucose from the liver and kidneys, and also causes symptoms of increased heart rate and blood pressure.

Essential fatty acids (EFAs)   Two classes of essential dietary fats that must be obtained from food or supplements. The two classes are Omega-3 and Omega-6, with the numbers designating the location of the first chemical double bond in the molecule.

Essential nutrients   Essential nutrients are nutrients that are required for life but the body cannot make internally. Hence, they must be obtained from the diet.

Exogenous   Sourced from outside the body; relating to, or developing from, external factors.

Fat   One of the three macronutrients; an organic compound that dissolves in other oils but not in water. A source of energy and building blocks of cells. Foods rich in fatty acids. There are three main types of fats found in food. Saturated fats are solid at room temperature and include butter, coconut oil, ghee, lard, and beef tallow. Monounsaturated fats include olive oil. Polyunsaturated fats include vegetable oils such as safflower, sunflower, and soybean oil.

Fat-adaptation   The process of becoming adapted to using ketones instead of glucose as the primary cellular fuel in the body. Also known as keto-adaptation.

Fatty acids   The scientific term for fat molecules in the body, which are part of a group of substances called lipids. Fatty acids come in different lengths from 6-carbon to 26-carbon chains.

Fiber   Parts of plant foods that are indigestible or very slowly digested, with little effect on blood sugar and insulin levels; sometimes called roughage.

Free radicals   Chemically unstable molecules that "steal" electrons from surrounding molecules. They are in the environment and naturally produced by our bodies. Excess free radicals can damage cells through oxidative activity. Think of what rust is to steel.

Fructosamine   A molecule formed from the joining of fructose to protein molecules in the blood through glycation. Tests for fructosamine are done when hemoglobin anomalies render the hemoglobin A1c test inconclusive.

Fructose   A simple sugar found naturally in fruits and plants. It is also found in commercial sweeteners such as high-fructose corn syrup and crystalline fructose. Excess intake of fructose has been implicated in many health issues.

GERD   Gastrointestinal-esophageal reflux disease. A medical term for severe heartburn.

Glucagon   A hormone secreted by the alpha cells of the pancreas, which signals the liver to break down stored glycogen into glucose and release it into the bloodstream to maintain normal blood-sugar levels.

Glucocorticoids   A class of steroid hormones that regulate or support a variety of important cardiovascular, metabolic, immunologic, and homeostatic functions in the body. For example, secretion of these hormones can raise low blood sugar, modulate inflammation, and promote cell growth.

Gluconeogenesis The process by which glucose is formed in the liver from a non-carbohydrate source when blood sugar is low.

Glucose A simple sugar that your cells use to make energy. It is created from the breakdown or metabolism of foods that contain carbohydrate (starches and sugars) and, to a lesser extent, protein foods such as meat and eggs.

Glucose intolerance Abnormal increase in blood glucose after a carbohydrate-containing meal or during an oral glucose-tolerance test (OGTT).

Glycation A process in which excess blood glucose bonds to or "sticks" to protein or fat molecules in body tissues, causing impairment of the glycated tissue. For example, nerve endings can become glycated and result in diabetic neuropathy (nerve pain). Glycation is like rubbing maple syrup on your hands and then trying to fold clothes or type on a keyboard.

Glycemic load The mathematical product of glycemic index and total carbohydrate content of a given food. Glycemic index is a measure of the blood-sugar increase after consuming a food containing 50 grams of carbohydrate compared to the blood-sugar increase from consuming 50 grams of glucose or white bread. The higher the glycemic index of a particular food, the higher the blood sugar rise in response to consuming that food.

Glycerol Glycerol is the "backbone" of a fatty acid or triglyceride. Imagine a capital E. The glycerol molecule represents the vertical spine of the E with fatty acids making up the horizontal lines of the E.

Glycogen The storage form of carbohydrate in the body.

Glycolysis The pathway by which glucose is broken down in the cell into two molecules of pyruvic acid with the generation of energy in the form of ATP.

Glycosuria A condition of glucose in the urine. It may be caused by kidney dysfunction or by the high blood sugars of diabetes.

Goal body weight (GBW) The weight you would like to attain, or the weight at which you feel best.

HbA1c Also known as glycated hemoglobin A1c, this is a test that measures average blood sugar over the past three months. It indicates to what level and time blood sugars have been elevated, because it measures the amount of "glycated" hemoglobin in red blood cells.

HDL cholesterol High-density lipoprotein; the "good" type of cholesterol.

Hepatic Coming from or having to do with the liver.

HFCS High-fructose corn syrup. Cheap sweetener used in soft drinks and other processed food products.

HHS Hyperglycemic hyperosmolar syndrome. HHS is the initial manifestation of diabetes in 7%–17% of patients. Infection is the major precipitating factor, occurring in 30%–60% of patients.

Homocysteine An amino acid that acts as a marker for heart disease. A high level of homocysteine in the blood (hyperhomocysteinemia) makes a person more prone to endothelial cell injury and inflammation in the blood vessels. This can increase the risk of atherosclerosis and heart attack.

High sensitivity C-Reactive protein (hs-CRP)   A test which measures inflammation in the body. Inflammation is a marker for tissue damage that can be caused by elevated blood glucose.

Honeymoon period   In a person who has type 1 diabetes (T1DM), immune cells destroy the insulin-producing beta cells in the pancreas. However, right after the time of diagnosis, some people go through a "honeymoon phase" in which their remaining beta cells still function, and the body is able to produce its own insulin.

Hydrogenated oils   Vegetable oils processed to a solid form to improve their shelf life. See trans fats.

Hyperglycemia   A metabolic state of elevated blood sugar, which can cause body damage through the actions of glycation.

Hyperglycemic glycosuria   A condition of excess sugar in the urine due to high levels of blood glucose.

Hyperinsulinemia   Condition of chronically elevated blood-insulin levels.

Hypertension   Medical term for high blood pressure. Blood pressure is a measurement of the force of blood against your blood vessels, and it is reported as two numbers (e.g., 140/90). The top number is the systolic pressure, which is a measure of pressure in the arteries when the heart beats and pushes more blood into the arteries. The second number, called the diastolic pressure, is the pressure in the arteries when the heart rests between beats. The ideal blood pressure for non-pregnant people with diabetes is 130/80 or less.

Hypoglycemia   A metabolic state of low blood sugar. Hypoglycemia can be associated with symptoms such as rapid heart rate, profuse sweating, flushing, and confusion, among others. It can also occur without symptoms, meaning that even though the measurement of blood sugar is low, no symptoms of low blood sugar are evident. The symptoms are caused by the brain's signal to the sympathetic nervous system and adrenal glands to release adrenaline (epinephrine), norepinephrine (the "fight or flight" hormones), and acetylcholine. These hormones normally signal the liver to break down stored sugar and release it into the bloodstream and to signal the person to seek out food and, in particular, glucose. When the symptoms of hypoglycemia are either impaired or absent, it can be dangerous, since the warning system is also absent. See hypoglycemia-associated autonomic failure (HAAF). glycemia-associated autonomic failure (HAAF).

Hypoglycemia-associated autonomic failure (HAAF)   HAAF occurs most commonly in persons with T1DM or advanced insulin-deficient T2DM who have experienced recent hypoglycemic episodes during sleep or after exercise. These episodes cause both defective glucose-counter regulation (in the absence of decrements in insulin and increments in glucagon) and hypoglycemic unawareness (reduction in the sympathoadrenal responses) and, therefore, a vicious cycle of recurrent hypoglycemia.

Hypoglycemic unawareness   A reduction in the sympathoadrenal response to low blood sugar. It is a complication of diabetes in which the patient is unaware of a deep drop in blood sugar because it fails to trigger the secretion of epinephrine which generates the characteristic symptoms of hypoglycemia (such as palpitations, sweating, anxiety) that serve to warn the patient of the dropping blood-sugar levels.

Hyperglycemic hyperosmolar syndrome (HHS)   Diabetic hyperglycemic hyperosmolar syndrome (HHS) is a complication of type 2 diabetes. It is characterized by extremely high blood-sugar levels without the presence of ketones.

Inflammation   Part of the body's delicately balanced natural defense system against potentially damaging substances. Excessive inflammation is associated with increased risk of heart attack, stroke, diabetes, and some forms of cancer.

Islet cell   Specialized cells in the pancreas that produce various endocrine hormones such as insulin, glucagon, somatostatin, ghrelin, and amylin.

Insulin   A hormone produced by the pancreas that signals cells to take up glucose and amino acids from the bloodstream. Insulin also blocks the release of fat from fat cells. Insulin is sourced and released from the pancreas (endogenous insulin) in proportion to the amount of glucose in the bloodstream. Insulin can also come from external or exogenous sources, such as insulin injections or pumps.

Insulin-like growth factor 1 (IGF-1)   A hormone secreted by the liver and similar in structure to insulin. IGF-1 is one of the most potent natural activators of the AKT signaling pathway, a stimulator of cell growth and proliferation, and a potent inhibitor of programmed cell death.

Insulinogenic   Relating to or causing the stimulation of the production of insulin.

Insulin resistance (IR)   A metabolic condition in which chronically high levels of circulating insulin result in body cells becoming desensitized and unable to respond properly to the insulin signal. Insulin's job is to push glucose from the bloodstream into cells, where it can be metabolized for energy. Without proper insulin signaling, glucose builds up in the blood, which then perpetuates further elevation of insulin levels. If left untreated, this circle of insulin and glucose elevation can lead to a diagnosis of metabolic syndrome and prediabetes and can develop into type 2 diabetes (T2DM).

Keto-adaptation   The process of becoming adapted to using ketones instead of glucose as the primary cellular fuel in the body. Also known as fat-adaptation.

Ketoacidosis   The uncontrolled overproduction of ketones characteristic of untreated type 1 diabetes, with ketones typically five to ten times higher than in nutritional ketosis.

Ketogenesis   The metabolic process in which the liver creates ketone bodies from the breakdown of fatty acids. The ketone bodies can then be metabolized within the cell mitochondria to fuel the body.

Ketogenic diet (KD)   A high-fat, moderate-protein, low-carbohydrate diet used to treat various illnesses and improve health through a change in cellular fuel metabolism.

Ketone bodies   A water soluble molecule produced by the liver from fatty acids during periods of low food intake (fasting) or carbohydrate restriction. They are used as an alternate energy source by various body cells and systems when glucose levels are low. The three ketone bodies are acetoacetate, beta-hydroxybutyrate and acetone.

Ketosis   A metabolic state where most of the body's energy supply comes from fat-derived ketone bodies in the blood, instead of coming from carbohydrate-derived glucose. Also known as nutritional ketosis.

Lactic acidosis   A condition in which lactic acid builds up in the bloodstream faster than it can be removed, which causes the blood to become too acidic.

Lactose   The simple sugar (carbohydrate) found in milk and milk products such as cheese and yogurt. In many studies, lactose has been shown to increase insulin out of proportion to the carbohydrate content.

LADA   The short term for latent autoimmune diabetes of adults. It is also called type 1.5 diabetes. A form of diabetes that is similar to type 1 diabetes but has a slow time period of development, and so it manifests in adulthood.

LCHF   Low carb, high fat.

LDL cholesterol   Low-density lipoprotein. Commonly known as the "bad" type of cholesterol. However, only the small, dense LDL particles that are associated with CVD are "bad." Small, dense LDL particles occur in persons with insulin resistance consuming refined carbohydrates.

Lean body mass (LBM)   Body mass minus fat tissue; includes muscle, bone, organs, and connective tissue.

Legumes   Most members of the bean and pea families, including lentils, chickpeas, soybeans, peas, and numerous others.

Lipid-heart hypothesis   The hypothesis that a high intake of saturated fat and elevated LDL cholesterol are the most important causes of atherosclerosis and coronary heart disease. Also known as the diet-heart hypothesis.

Lipids   Lipids constitute a group of naturally occurring molecules that include fats, waxes, sterols (such as cholesterol), fat-soluble vitamins (such as vitamins A, D, E, and K), monoglycerides, diglycerides, triglycerides, phospholipids, and others. The main biological functions of lipids include storage of energy, signaling, and acting as structural components of cell membranes.

Lipoprotein (a)   Lipoprotein(a), also known as Lp(A), is a subclass of LDL cholesterol. High Lp(a) blood levels are a risk factor for coronary heart disease (CHD), stroke, atherosclerosis, thrombosis, and stroke. High Lp(a) levels also predict risk of early atherosclerosis independently of other cardiac risk factors, including LDL.

Macronutrients   The three main types of nutrients in the diet: fat, protein, and carbohydrate.

Macrophages   A type of white blood cell that engulfs and digests cellular debris, foreign substances, microbes, and cancer cells in an immune system process called phagocytosis.

Medium-chain triglycerides (MCTs)   MCTs are fatty acids with 6 to 10 carbon atoms, which are more rapidly absorbed from the intestine compared to long-chain triglycerides. In addition, MCTs do not require intestinal bile salts for digestion. Individuals who have malnutrition or digestive absorption issues are treated with MCTs because they don't require energy for absorption and utilization in the body, and they increase ketone production, especially in persons following a ketogenic diet.

Multi-dose injections (MDI)   Multiple dose injection (MDI) therapy, also known as multiple daily injections, is an alternate term for the basal/bolus regime of injecting insulin. The therapy involves injecting a long-acting insulin once or twice daily as a background (basal) dose and having further injections of rapid-acting insulin at each mealtime.

Metabolic syndrome   A group of conditions, including hypertension, high triglycerides, low HDL cholesterol, higher-than-normal blood sugar and insulin levels, and weight carried in the middle of the body. Also known as syndrome X or insulin resistance syndrome, it predisposes you to various diseases.

Metabolism   The complex chemical processes that convert food into energy or the body's building blocks, which, in turn, become part of organs, tissues, and cells.

mg/dL   Stands for milligrams per deciliter. It's a unit of measure that shows the concentration of a substance in a specific amount of fluid. It is used as a standard measurement of blood sugar in test results.

Mitochondria   Cell organelles called the "cellular power plants" because they generate most of the cell's supply of adenosine triphosphate (ATP), the main form of cellular energy.

mM or mmol/L   Stands for millimolar. A unit of measurement that represents a concentration of one thousandth of a solute mole per liter. Ketone levels in blood can be measured and reported in mM.

Monounsaturated fatty acids (MUFA)   A type of dietary fat typically found in foods such as olive oil, canola oil, nuts, and avocados, but also beef steak.

Monosodium glutamate (MSG)   A chemical used to heighten taste sensations in processed foods. MSG is a neurotoxin and should be avoided on a ketogenic diet because it contains glutamate, a derivate of glutamine.

Myocardial infarction   Medical term for a heart attack, which occurs when blood flow to the heart is compromised, and the lack of oxygen injures the heart muscle.

Myocardium   The muscular tissue of the heart.

NAFLD   Non-alcoholic fatty liver disease.

Nephropathy   Kidney disease; damage or disease that affects the kidneys.

Neuropathy   Damage to or disease affecting nerves, which may impair sensation, movement, gland or organ function, or other aspects of health, depending on the type of nerve affected. See also *peripheral neuropathy.*

Non-alcoholic fatty liver disease (NAFLD)   Non-alcoholic fatty liver disease (NAFLD) is the build-up of extra fat in the liver. NAFLD is associated with insulin resistance and metabolic syndrome, and it tends to develop more readily when the diet is high in sugars and fructose and low in choline.

Nutrient   A nutrient is a chemical that an organism needs to live and grow. Nutrients are used to build and repair tissues and regulate body processes, and they can be converted for use as energy substrates. Fats, proteins, carbohydrates, vitamins, minerals, and water are nutrients for humans.

Nutritional ketosis   The moderate and controlled level of ketones in the bloodstream that allows the body to function well with little dietary carbohydrate. A state of ketosis that is safe and normal when carbohydrate or calories are restricted.

OGTT   Oral glucose-tolerance test. A medical test in which a large amount of glucose is given with blood samples taken afterward to see how quickly the glucose is cleared from the blood.

Omega-3 fatty acids   A group of essential polyunsaturated fats found in green algae, cold-water fish, fish oil, flaxseed oil, and some other nut and vegetable oils. Omega-3 fatty acids have an anti-inflammatory effect on body systems.

Omega-6 fatty acids   A group of essential polyunsaturated fats found in many vegetable oils and also in meats from animals fed corn, soybeans, and certain other vegetable products. Omega-6 fatty acids have an inflammatory downstream effect on body systems.

Oxidative stress   The condition in which the production of reactive oxygen species (ROS) through various metabolic pathways is at a greater rate than the body's defense system of antioxidants can handle, resulting in cellular damage at the molecular level. Oxidative stress is thought to play a part in many disease processes.

Partially hydrogenated oil   Oil that has been solidified using a catalytic chemical manufacturing process. See trans fats.

Peripheral neuropathy   Nerve damage caused by chronically high blood sugar. It leads to numbness, loss of sensation, and sometimes pain in the feet, legs, or hands. It is the most common complication of diabetes.

Plaque   A buildup in the arteries of cholesterol, fat, calcium, and other substances that can block blood flow and result in a heart attack or stroke.

Polycystic ovary syndrome (PCOS)   A common endocrine-system disorder among women of reproductive age. Symptoms include Infrequent or prolonged menstrual periods, excess hair growth, acne, and obesity. Women with PCOS tend to be insulin resistant as well.

Polydipsia   Excessive thirst.

Polyunsaturated fatty acids (PUFA)   Fats with a chemical structure that keeps them liquid in the cold; oils from corn, soybean, sunflower, safflower, cottonseed, grape seed, flaxseed, sesame seed, some nuts, and fatty fish are typically high in polyunsaturated fat.

Polyuria   Excessive urination.

Postprandial   Medical term for "after a meal."

Prediabetes   A condition in which blood sugar levels are higher than normal but fall short of full-blown diabetes.

Protein   One of the three macronutrients found in food, used for energy and to build cells and tissues. Proteins are made up of chains of amino acids. Examples are meats, poultry, fish, shellfish, tofu, and whey.

RDA (recommended daily allowance)   The average daily dietary intake level of a nutrient that is sufficient to meet the required amount of that nutrient in nearly all healthy individuals (approximately 98%).

Reactive hypoglycemia   An episode of symptomatic low blood sugar which occurs about 4 hours after consuming a high-carbohydrate meal. In response to the blood-sugar spike caused by the large influx of carbohydrate, the pancreas releases an excessive surge of insulin which drives blood-glucose levels below the pre-meal baseline.

Reactive oxygen species   Chemically reactive molecules containing oxygen, which when produced in large amounts in the cell plasma and mitochondrial electron transport chain, can cause oxidative damage to cellular DNA and other structures and result in cell death.

Resistance exercise   Any exercise that builds muscle strength; also called weight-bearing, weight lifting, or anaerobic exercise.

ROS   Reactive oxygen species.

rt-CGM   Real-time continuous glucose monitor. See CGM.

SAD   Standard American diet, which is high in carbohydrate and lower in fat.

Satiety   A pleasurable sense of fullness.

Saturated fatty acids (SFA)   Fatty acids that are solid at room temperature; the majority of fat in butter, lard, suet, palm, and coconut oil.

Serum blood sugar   Blood sugar measured from centrifuged blood taken and processed in a lab, as opposed to a whole-blood measurement done at home.

Substrate   In chemistry, a substance that is acted upon in a biochemical reaction, or a substance used or needed to create a new molecule.

Sucrose   Table sugar; sucrose is composed of two monosaccharides or simple sugars called glucose and fructose.

Sugar alcohols   Sweeteners such as glycerin, mannitol, erythritol, sorbitol, and xylitol that typically have little or no impact on blood sugar. They are, however, anti-ketogenic in that they interfere with ketosis.

Symptomatic   Having symptoms.

T1DM (type 1 diabetes)   Type 1 diabetes mellitus, or insulin-dependent diabetes mellitus (IDDM), formerly known as juvenile diabetes because it was mostly found in children. An autoimmune disease in which the cells that secrete insulin in the pancreas have been damaged or destroyed. The result is that the body is unable to make insulin, so the insulin must be supplied from external sources.

T2DM (type 2 diabetes)   Type 2 diabetes mellitus, or non-insulin-dependent diabetes mellitus (NIDDM). This condition was formerly known as adult-onset diabetes because it was rarely found in children. In contrast to T1DM, type 2 manifests due to insulin resistance. The pancreas may still produce insulin, but cells have become resistant to insulin's message. In other words, the cells cannot "hear" the insulin asking to move sugar into the cells. As a result, the body cannot respond to insulin requests to move blood sugar into the cells, and the sugar in the bloodstream rises to damaging levels.

T-cell   A type of white blood cell called a lymphocyte, which is part of the human immune system. There are several different kinds, each with a distinct immune system function.

Thiazide   A type of molecule and a class of diuretic often used to treat hypertension (high blood pressure) and edema or swelling such as caused by heart or kidney disease.

Titrate   To gradually increase the dose of a drug until it reaches maximum effectiveness, not necessarily the maximum dose.

Trans fats (TFA)   Trans fatty acids or trans fats are found in hydrogenated or partially hydrogenated vegetable oil, typically used in fried foods, baked goods, and other products. A high intake of trans fats is associated with increased risk of heart attack.

Triglycerides   The major form of fat that circulates in the bloodstream in VLDL and LDL particles and is stored as body fat. A high-carbohydrate diet increases triglycerides. Triglycerides are used as an energy source in addition to glucose; however, chronically elevated levels of triglycerides are associated with greater risks for heart disease and are a marker for insulin resistance and metabolic syndrome.

Unsaturated fat   Monounsaturated fats such as olive oil and polyunsaturated fats found in most vegetable and fish oils. They are usually liquid at room temperature.

VLDL cholesterol   Very-low-density lipoprotein. Molecules secreted by the liver that enable fats and cholesterol to move within the water-based solution of the bloodstream.

Math Symbols

<	less than
>	greater than
≠	not equal to
≤	less than or equal to
≥	greater than or equal to
±	plus or minus

Endnotes

1 Newburgh LH, Marsh PL. The use of a high fat diet in the treatment of diabetes mellitus: second paper: blood sugar. *Arch Intern Med* (chic). 1921;27(6):699-705.

2 Center for Disease Control webpage on diabetes statistics and data. Available at http://www.cdc.gov/diabetes/data/statistics/2014StatisticsReport.html

3 Cahill GF, Jr. Fuel metabolism in starvation. *Annu Rev Nutr.* 2006;26:1-22. Review.

4 Veech RL. The therapeutic implications of ketone bodies: the effects of ketone bodies in pathological conditions: ketosis, ketogenic diet, redox states, insulin resistance, and mitochondrial metabolism. *Prostaglandins Leukot Essent Fatty Acids.* 2004 Mar;70(3):309--9. Review.

5 Yamagishi, S, Matsui, T. (2010). Advanced glycation end products, oxidative stress and diabetic nephropathy. *Oxidative Medicine and Cellular Longevity,* 3(2), 101–108. doi:10.4161/oxim.3.2.4.

6 Ahsan H. Diabetic retinopathy: Biomolecules and multiple pathophysiology. *Diabetes Metab Syndr.* 2015 January–March;9(1):51–54.

7 Sandireddy R, Yerra VG, Areti A, Komirishetty P, Kumar A. Neuroinflammation and oxidative stress in diabetic neuropathy: futuristic strategies based on these targets. *Int J Endocrinol.* 2014;2014:674987.

8 Yamagishi S. Advanced glycation end products and receptor-oxidative stress system in diabetic vascular complications. *Ther Apher Dial.* 2009 Dec;13(6):534-9.

9 Paoli A, Rubini A, Volek JS, Grimaldi KA. Beyond weight loss: a review of the therapeutic uses of very-low-carbohydrate (ketogenic) diets. *Eur J Clin Nutr.* 2013 Aug;67(8):789-96.

10 Feinman, RD, Pogozelski WK, Astrup A, Bernstein RK, Fine EJ, et al. Dietary carbohydrate restriction as the first approach in diabetes management: critical review and evidence base. *Nutrition.* 2015 Jan;31(1):1-13.

11 Center for Disease Control webpage on diabetes statistics and data. Available at http://www.cdc.gov/diabetes/data/statistics/2014StatisticsReport.html.

12 Although not discussed in this book, additional types of diabetes include gestational diabetes, a form of glucose intolerance (abnormal increase in blood glucose after a carbohydrate-containing meal or during an oral glucose-tolerance test) diagnosed during the second or third trimester of pregnancy, and type 3 diabetes, also known as Alzheimer's disease. See reference paper available at http://www.ncbi.nlm.nih.gov/pubmed/25088942.

13 Eades, M. A Spoonful of Sugar. Protein Power blog. Available http://www.proteinpower.com/drmike/sugar-and-sweeteners/a-spoonful-of-sugar/

14 Symons TB, Schutzler SE, Cocke TL, Chinkes DL, Wolfe RR, Paddon-Jones D. Aging does not impair the anabolic response to a protein-rich meal. *Am J Clin Nutr.* 2007 Aug;86(2):451-6.

15 Nielsen JV, Gando C, Joensson E, Paulsson C. Low carbohydrate diet in type 1 diabetes, long-term improvement and adherence: A clinical audit. *Diabetol Metab Syndr.* 2012 May 31;4(1):23.

16 Dashti HM, Mathew TC, Khadada M, Al-Mousawi M, Talib H, Asfar SK, Behbahani AI, Al-Zaid NS. Beneficial effects of ketogenic diet in obese diabetic subjects. *Mol Cell Biochem.* 2007 Aug;302(1--2):249--56. Epub 2007 Apr 20.

17 Forsythe CE, Phinney SD, Fernandez ML, Quann EE, Wood RJ, Bibus DM, Kraemer WJ, Feinman RD, Volek JS. Comparison of low-fat and low-carbohydrate diets on circulating fatty acid composition and markers of inflammation. *Lipids.* 2008 Jan;43(1):65--77.

18 Austin GL, Thiny MT, Westman EC, Yancy WS Jr, Shaheen NJ. A very low-carbohydrate diet improves gastroesophageal reflux and its symptoms. *Dig Dis Sci.* 2006 Aug;51(8):1307--12. Epub 2006 Jul 27.

19 Struzycka I. The oral microbiome in dental caries. *Pol J Microbiol.* 2014;63(2):127–35. Review.

20 Phelps JR, Siemers SV, El-Mallakh RS. The ketogenic diet for type II bipolar disorder. *Neurocase.* 2013;19(5):423--6.

21 Kraft BD, Westman EC. Schizophrenia, gluten, and low-carbohydrate, ketogenic diets: a case report and review of the literature. *Nutr Metab (Lond).* 2009 Feb 26;6:10.

22 Giovannucci E. Metabolic syndrome, hyperinsulinemia, and colon cancer: a review. *Am J Clin Nutr.* 2007 Sep;86(3):s836--42. Review.

23 Browning JD, Baker JA, Rogers T, Davis J, Satapati S, Burgess SC. Short-term weight loss and hepatic triglyceride reduction: evidence of a metabolic advantage with dietary carbohydrate restriction. *Am J Clin Nutr.* 2011 May;93(5):1048-52.

24 Siri-Tarino PW, Sun Q, Hu FB, Krauss RM. Meta-analysis of prospective cohort studies evaluating the association of saturated fat with cardiovascular disease. *Am J Clin Nutr.* 2010 Mar;91(3):535–46.

25 Gardner CD, Kiazand A, Alhassan S, Kim S, Stafford RS, Balise RR, Kraemer HC, King AC. Comparison of the Atkins, Zone, Ornish, and LEARN diets for change in weight and related risk factors among overweight premenopausal women: the A TO Z Weight Loss Study: a randomized trial. *JAMA.* 2007 Mar 7;297(9):969–77. Erratum in: JAMA. 2007 Jul 11;298(2):178.

26 Sharman MJ, Kraemer WJ, Love DM, Avery NG, Gómez AL, Scheett TP, Volek JS. A ketogenic diet favorably affects serum biomarkers for cardiovascular disease in normal-weight men. *J Nutr.* 2002 Jul;132(7):1879–85.

27 Porter FD. Smith-Lemli-Opitz syndrome: pathogenesis, diagnosis and management. *Eur J Hum Genet.* 2008 May;16(5):535–41.

28 Chowdhury R, Warnakula S, Kunutsor S, Crowe F, Ward HA, et al. Association of dietary, circulating, and supplement fatty acids with coronary risk: a systematic review and meta-analysis. *Ann Intern Med.* 2014 Mar 18;160(6):398–406. Review. Erratum in: *Ann Intern Med.* 2014 May 6;160(9):658.

29 Khaw KT, Wareham N, Luben R, Bingham S, Oakes S, Welch A, Day N. Glycated haemoglobin, diabetes, and mortality in men in Norfolk cohort of european prospective investigation of cancer and nutrition (EPIC-Norfolk). *BMJ*. 2001 Jan 6;322(7277):15–8.

30 Siri-Tarino PW, Sun Q, Hu FB, Krauss RM. Saturated fat, carbohydrate, and cardiovascular disease. *Am J Clin Nutr*. 2010;91(3):502–509.

31 Dietary Reference Intakes for Energy, Carbohydrate, Fiber, Fat, Fatty Acids, Cholesterol, Protein, and Amino Acids (Macronutrients) (2005). *The National Academies Press*. Available at http://www.nap.edu/catalog/10490/dietary-reference-intakes-for-energy-carbohydrate-fiber-fat-fatty-acids-cholesterol-protein-and-amino-acids-macronutrients.

32 Chase P, Maahs D. Understanding Diabetes, Chapter 12: Food Management and Diabetes. University of Colorado School of Medicine. Barbara Davis Center for Diabetes. Available at http://www.ucdenver.edu/academics/colleges/medicalschool/centers/BarbaraDavis/OnlineBooks/Pages/default.aspx.

33 Foundations of Care: Education, Nutrition, Physical Activity, Smoking Cessation, Psychosocial Care, and Immunization. American Diabetes Association Position Statement. Available at http://care.diabetesjournals.org/content/38/Supplement_1/S20.full.pdf.

34 Carbohydrate Counting. American Diabetes Association. Available at http://www.diabetes.org/food-and-fitness/food/what-can-i-eat/understanding-carbohydrates/carbohydrate-counting.html

35 Marcovecchio ML, Heywood JJ, Dalton RN, Dunger DB. The contribution of glycemic control to impaired growth during puberty in young people with type 1 diabetes and microalbuminuria. *Pediatr Diabetes*. 2014 Jun;15(4):303–8.

36 Pater A, Sypniewska G, Pilecki O. Biochemical markers of bone cell activity in children with type 1 diabetes mellitus. *J Pediatr Endocrinol Metab*. 2010 Jan–Feb;23(1–2):81–6.

37 Neumann CG, Harrison GG. Onset and evolution of stunting in infants and children. Examples from the Human Nutrition Collaborative Research Support Program. Kenya and Egypt studies. *Eur J Clin Nutr*. 1994 Feb;48 Suppl 1:S90-102. Review.

38 Nansel TR, Lipsky LM, Liu A. Greater diet quality is associated with more optimal glycemic control in a longitudinal study of youth with type 1 diabetes. *Am J Clin Nutr*. 2016 Jul;104(1):81–7. Epub 2016 May 18.

39 Kossoff EH, Freeman JM, Turner Z, Rubenstein JE. *Ketogenic diets: treatments for epilepsy and other disorders. 5th edition*. New York: Demos; 2011.

40 Tack C, Pohlmeier H, Behnke T, et al. Accuracy Evaluation of Five Blood Glucose Monitoring Systems Obtained from the Pharmacy: A European Multicenter Study with 453 Subjects. *Diabetes Technology & Therapeutics*. 2012;14(4):330–337.

41 Rosedale, Ron. Cholesterol is Not the Cause of Heart Disease article. Available at http://drrosedale.com/Cholesterol_is_NOT_the_cause_of_heart_disease.htm#axzz2SrJlxxHT

42 Campbell-McBride N. Cholesterol, Friend or Foe? Article available at http://www.westonaprice.org/health-topics/cholesterol-friend-or-foe/.

43 Salas-Salvadó J, Casas-Agustench P, Murphy MM, López-Uriarte P, Bulló M. The effect of nuts on inflammation. *Asia Pac J Clin Nutr.* 2008;17 Suppl 1:333-6.Review.

44 Cordain L, Miller JB, Eaton SB, Mann N, Holt SH, Speth JD. Plant-animal subsistence ratios and macronutrient energy estimations in worldwide hunter-gatherer diets. *Am J Clin Nutr.* 2000 Mar;71(3):682–92.

45 Boden et al. Effect of a low-carbohydrate diet on appetite, blood glucose levels, and insulin resistance in obese patients with type 2 diabetes. *Ann Intern Med.* 2005 Mar 15;142(6):403–11.

46 Meijer K, de Vos P, Priebe MG. Butyrate and other short-chain fatty acids as modulators of immunity: what relevance for health? *Curr Opin Clin Nutr Metab Care.* 2010 Nov;13(6):715-21.

47 Marlett JA, Fischer MH. The active fraction of psyllium seed husk. *Proc Nutr Soc.* 2003 Feb;62(1):207-9. Review.

48 Davis E. Sugar Alcohols article. Ketogenic Diet Resource. Available at http://www.ketogenic-diet-resource.com/sugar-alcohol.html.

49 CI Medical Center website. Available at http://www.cimedicalcenter.com/metabolism-p124

50 Chandalia M, Garg A, Lutjohann D, von Bergmann K, Grundy SM, Brinkley LJ. Beneficial effects of high dietary fiber intake in patients with type 2 diabetes mellitus. *N Engl J Med.* 2000 May 11;342(19):1392-8.

51 Hebert SL, Nair KS. Protein and Energy Metabolism in Type 1 Diabetes. *Clinical Nutrition* (Edinburgh, Scotland). 2010;29(1):13.

52 Stenström G, Gottsäter A, Bakhtadze E, Berger B, Sundkvist G. Latent autoimmune diabetes in adults: definition, prevalence, beta-cell function, and treatment. *Diabetes.* 2005 Dec;54 Suppl 2:S68-72.

53 Rewers M, Gottlieb P. Immunotherapy for the Prevention and Treatment of Type 1 Diabetes: Human trials and a look into the future. *Diabetes Care.* 2009;32(10):1769–1782.

54 A1C Goals, Glycemic Targets, Standards of Medical Care in Diabetes 2017. American Diabetes Association Position Statement. Available at http://care.diabetesjournals.org/content/40/Supplement_1/S48

55 Nielsen JV, Gando C, Joensson E, Paulsson C. Low carbohydrate diet in type 1 diabetes, long-term improvement and adherence: A clinical audit. *Diabetol Metab Syndr.* 2012 May 31;4(1):23.

56 Bell, Kirstine J et al. Efficacy of carbohydrate counting in type 1 diabetes: a systematic review and meta-analysis. *The Lancet Diabetes & Endocrinology*, Volume 2, Issue 2, 133–140.

57 Laurenzi A, Bolla AM, Panigoni G, et al. Effects of Carbohydrate Counting on Glucose Control and Quality of Life Over 24 Weeks in Adult Patients With Type 1 Diabetes on Continuous Subcutaneous Insulin Infusion: A randomized, prospective clinical trial (GIOCAR). *Diabetes Care.* 2011;34(4):823–827. doi:10.2337/dc10-1490.

58 Unger RH, Cherrington AD. Glucagonocentric restructuring of diabetes: a pathophysiologic and therapeutic makeover. *J Clin Invest.* 2012 Jan;122(1):4-12.

59 Heinemann L, Weyer C, Rauhaus M, Heinrichs S, Heise T. Variability of the metabolic effect of soluble insulin and the rapid-acting insulin analog insulin aspart. *Diabetes Care.* 1998 Nov;21(11):1910–4.

60 Yeh HC, Brown TT, Maruthur N, Ranasinghe P, Berger Z, Suh YD, Wilson LM, Haberl EB, Brick J, Bass EB, Golden SH. Comparative effectiveness and safety of methods of insulin delivery and glucose monitoring for diabetes mellitus: a systematic review and meta-analysis. *Ann Intern Med.* 2012 Sep 4;157(5):336–47.

61 Poolsup N, Suksomboon N, Kyaw AM. Systematic review and meta-analysis of the effectiveness of continuous glucose monitoring (CGM) on glucose control in diabetes. *Diabetology & Metabolic Syndrome.* 2013;5:39.

62 Battelino T, Phillip M, Bratina N, Nimri R, Oskarsson P, Bolinder J. Effect of continuous glucose monitoring on hypoglycemia in type 1 diabetes. *Diabetes Care.* 2011 Apr;34(4):795–800. Epub 2011 Feb 19.

63 American Diabetes Association. Classification and diagnosis of diabetes. Sec. 2. In Standards of Medical Care in Diabetes - 2015. *Diabetes Care* 2015;38(Suppl. 1):S8–S16.

64 American Association Of Clinical Endocrinologists and American College Of Endocrinology Clinical Practice Guidelines For Developing A Diabetes Mellitus Comprehensive Care Plan – 2015. *Endocr Pract.* 2015;21(Suppl 1).

65 Martin-Timon I., Del Canizo-Gomez F.J. Mechanisms of hypoglycemia unawareness and implications in diabetic patients. *World J. Diabetes.* 2015;6:912–926.

66 Borg R, Kuenen JC, Carstensen B, et al. HbA1c and mean blood glucose show stronger associations with cardiovascular disease risk factors than do postprandial glycaemia or glucose variability in persons with diabetes: the A1C-Derived Average Glucose (ADAG) study. *Diabetologia.* 2011;54(1):69–72.

67 Daly ME, Vale C, Walker M, Littlefield A, Alberti KG, Mathers JC. Acute effects on insulin sensitivity and diurnal metabolic profiles of a high-sucrose compared with a high-starch diet. *Am J Clin Nutr.* 1998 Jun;67(6):1186–96.

68 Goldin A, Beckman JA, Schmidt AM, Creager MA. Advanced glycation end products: sparking the development of diabetic vascular injury. *Circulation.* 2006 Aug 8;114(6):597–605. Review.

69 Forbes JM, Cooper ME. Glycation in diabetic nephropathy. *Amino Acids.* 2012 Apr;42(4):1185–92. Epub 2010 Oct 21. Review.

70 Sugimoto K, Yasujima M, Yagihashi S. Role of advanced glycation end products in diabetic neuropathy. *Curr Pharm Des.* 2008;14(10):953–61. Review.

71 Stitt AW. The role of advanced glycation in the pathogenesis of diabetic retinopathy. *Exp Mol Pathol.* 2003 Aug;75(1):95–108. Review.

72 The effect of intensive treatment of diabetes on the development and progression of long-term complications in insulin-dependent diabetes mellitus. The Diabetes Control and Complications Trial Research Group. *N Engl J Med.* 1993 Sep 30;329(14):977–86.

73 Koga M, Kasayama S. Clinical impact of glycated albumin as another glycemic control marker. *Endocr J.* 2010;57(9):751–62. Epub 2010 Aug 17. Review.

74 390 Drugs that Affect Blood Sugar. Diabetes in Control website. Available at http://www.diabetesincontrol.com/tools/tools-for-your-practice/9625-drugs-that-can-affect-blood-glucose-levels.

75 CI Medical Center Metabolism and BMR Calculator. Available at http://www.cimedicalcenter.com/metabolism-calculating-your-bmr-bmi-p124.

76 Sapir DG, Owen OE. Renal conservation of ketone bodies during starvation. *Metabolism.* 1975 Jan;24(1):23–33.

77 Schwartz RM, Boyes S, Aynsley-Green A. Metabolic effects of three ketogenic diets in the treatment of severe epilepsy. *Dev Med Child Neurol.* 1989 Apr;31(2):152–60.

78 Reichard GA Jr, Owen OE, Haff AC, Paul P, Bortz WM. Ketone-body production andoxidation in fasting obese humans. *J Clin Invest.* 1974 Feb;53(2):508-15.

79 Comparison of Insulin Preparations. Camden Health website. Available at https://www.camdenhealth.org/wp-content/uploads/2011/03/Insulin_Preparation-3-14-11.pdf

80 Stewart WJ, McSweeney SM, Kellett MA, Faxon DP, Ryan TJ. Increased risk of severe protamine reactions in NPH insulin-dependent diabetics undergoing cardiac catheterization. *Circulation.* 1984 Nov;70(5):788–92.

81 De Leeuw I, Vague P, Selam JL, Skeie S, Lang H, Draeger E, Elte JW. Insulin detemir used in basal-bolus therapy in people with type 1 diabetes is associated with a lower risk of nocturnal hypoglycaemia and less weight gain over 12 months in comparison to NPH insulin. *Diabetes Obes Metab.* 2005 Jan;7(1):73–82.

82 Søeborg T, Rasmussen CH, Mosekilde E, Colding-Jørgensen M. Bioavailability and variability of biphasic insulin mixtures. *Eur J Pharm Sci.* 2012 Jul 16;46(4):198–208. Epub 2011 Jun 16. Review.

83 Marran KJ, Davey B, Lang A, Segal DG. Exponential increase in postprandial blood-glucose exposure with increasing carbohydrate loads using a linear carbohydrate-to-insulin ratio. *S Afr Med J.* 2013 Apr 10;103(7):461-3

84 Bell, Kirstine J et al. Efficacy of carbohydrate counting in type 1 diabetes: a systematic review and meta-analysis. *The Lancet Diabetes & Endocrinology*, Volume 2, Issue 2, 133–140.

85 Bergenstal RM, Johnson M, Powers MA, Wynne A, Vlajnic A, Hollander P, Rendell M. Adjust to target in type 2 diabetes: comparison of a simple algorithm with carbohydrate counting for adjustment of mealtime insulin glulisine. *Diabetes Care.* 2008 Jul;31(7):1305–10.

86 Johnson SR, Cooper MN, Jones TW, Davis EA. Long-term outcome of insulin pump therapy in children with type 1 diabetes assessed in a large population-based case-control study. *Diabetologia.* 2013 Nov;56(11):2392–400. Epub 2013 Aug 21.

87 Plank J, Bodenlenz M, Sinner F, Magnes C, Görzer E, Regittnig W, Endahl LA, Draeger E, Zdravkovic M, Pieber TR. A double-blind, randomized, dose-response study investigating the pharmacodynamic and pharmacokinetic properties of the long-acting insulin analog detemir. *Diabetes Care.* 2005 May;28(5):1107–12.

88 Layman DK. Dietary Guidelines should reflect new understandings about adult protein needs. *Nutrition & Metabolism.* 2009;6:12.

89 Volek JS, Phinney SD, Forsythe CE, Quann EE, Wood RJ, Puglisi MJ, Kraemer WJ, Bibus DM, Fernandez ML, Feinman RD. Carbohydrate restriction has a more favorable impact on the metabolic syndrome than a low fat diet. *Lipids.* 2009 Apr;44(4):297–309.

90 Borghouts LB, Keizer HA. Exercise and insulin sensitivity: a review. *Int J Sports Med.* 2000 Jan;21(1):1–12. Review.

91 King DS, Baldus PJ, Sharp RL, Kesl LD, Feltmeyer TL, Riddle MS. Time course for exercise-induced alterations in insulin action and glucose tolerance in middle-aged people. *J Appl Physiol* (1985). 1995 Jan;78(1):17–22.

92 Misbin RI. The phantom of lactic acidosis due to metformin in patients with diabetes. *Diabetes Care.* 2004 Jul;27(7):1791–3. Review.

93 Meyer L, Bohme P, Delbachian I, Lehert P, Cugnardey N, Drouin P, Guerci B. The benefits of metformin therapy during continuous subcutaneous insulin infusion treatment of type 1 diabetic patients. *Diabetes Care.* 2002 Dec;25(12):2153–8.

94 Vella S, Buetow L, Royle P, Livingstone S, Colhoun HM, Petrie JR. The use of metformin in type 1 diabetes: a systematic review of efficacy. *Diabetologia.* 2010 May;53(5):809–20.

95 Harrison LB, Mora PF, Clark GO, Lingvay I. Type 1 diabetes treatment beyond insulin: role of GLP-1 analogs. *J Investig Med.* 2013 Jan;61(1):40–4.

96 Lee NJ, Norris SL, Thakurta S. Efficacy and Harms of the Hypoglycemic Agent Pramlintide in Diabetes Mellitus. *Annals of Family Medicine.* 2010;8(6):542–549.

97 Rosenstock J, Ferrannini E. Euglycemic Diabetic Ketoacidosis: A Predictable, Detectable, and Preventable Safety Concern With SGLT2 Inhibitors. *Diabetes Care.* 2015 Sep;38(9):1638-42.

98 Lumb A. Diabetes and exercise. *Clinical Medicine* 2014; 14 (6): 63–6.

99 Dhaliwal SS, Welborn TA, Howat PA. Recreational Physical Activity as an Independent Predictor of Multivariable Cardiovascular Disease Risk. Moro C, ed. *PLoS ONE.* 2013;8(12):e83435.

100 Volek, Jeff S. et al. Metabolic characteristics of keto-adapted ultra-endurance runners. *Metabolism - Clinical and Experimental* , Volume 65 , Issue 3 , 100 – 110.

101 Phinney SD, Bistrian BR, Wolfe RR, Blackburn GL. The human metabolic response to chronic ketosis without caloric restriction: physical and biochemical adaptation. *Metabolism.* 1983 Aug;32(8):757–68.

102 Timothy Allen Olson website. Available at http://www.timothyallenolson.com/tag/western-states/.

103 Zach Bittern website. Available at http://zachbitterrunning.blogspot.com/p/results.html.

104 Emanuele NV, Swade TF, Emanuele MA. Consequences of alcohol use in diabetics. *Alcohol Health Res World.* 1998;22(3):211–9. Review.

Acknowledgments

Many thanks to Miriam Kalamian, both for her assistance and her expertise in implementing ketogenic diets and for being a good friend and mentor. Thanks also to Amy Berger for her friendship and for her time, knowledge, and suggestions for improving this book. Thanks also go to editor Annie Jo Smith for her excellent work and suggestions, and to Dr. Keith Runyan, whose contributions have made this a truly unique and useful book.

We also thank all of the researchers and other authors who are working to bring the truth about the efficacy of treating diabetes with a low-carb ketogenic diet to the public, despite the resistance of national diabetes organizations and pharmaceutical companies. My thanks go to Richard D. Feinman, PhD; Wendy K. Pogozelski, PhD; Arne Astrup, MD; Richard K. Bernstein, MD; Eugene J. Fine, MS, MD; Eric C. Westman, MD, MHS; Anthony Accurso, MD; Lynda Frassetto, MD; Barbara A. Gower, PhD; Samy I. McFarlane, MD; Jörgen Vesti Nielsen, MD; Thure Krarup, MD; Laura Saslow, PhD; Karl S. Roth, MD; Mary C. Vernon, MD; Jeff S. Volek, RD, PhD; Gilbert B. Wilshire, MD; Annika Dahlqvist, MD; Ralf Sundberg, MD, PhD; Ann Childers, MD; Katharine Morrison, MRCGP; Anssi H. Manninen, MHS; Hussain M. Dashti, MD, PhD, FACS, FICS; Richard J. Wood, PhD; Jay Wortman, MD; Stephen D. Phinney, MD, PhD; Nicolai Worm, PhD; Gary Taubes; Peter Attia, MD; Jeff Gerber, MD; Andreas Eenfeldt, MD; David Mendosa; Ron Rosedale, MD; Jenny Ruhl; and Jason Fung, MD.

Finally, thank you to everyone spends time reading our websites and books. We appreciate your attention, and hope the information helps you to achieve excellent health.

About the Authors

Ellen Davis has a Master's degree in Applied Clinical Nutrition from New York Chiropractic College. She created Ketogenic-Diet-Resource.com, a website showcasing the research on the positive health effects of ketogenic diets. Ellen has written articles for Well Being Journal, Terry's Naturally magazine and Healthy Living magazine, and authored several other books, including her book *Conquer Type 2 Diabetes with a Ketogenic Diet*, also coauthored with Keith Runyan, MD. In addition, her book *Fight Cancer with a Ketogenic Diet* is helping cancer patients utilize a ketogenic diet as therapy in over 70 countries.

Keith Runyan is medical doctor who has practiced clinical medicine in the areas of emergency medicine, internal medicine, nephrology, and obesity medicine. In 1998, he was diagnosed with type 1 diabetes and subsequently followed the conventional advice to treat his condition for the next 14 years. Although his glycemic control was at "recommended levels" of HbA1c of 6.5-7%, he was disturbed by frequent hypoglycemic episodes. After starting regular exercise to train for triathlons in 2007, his glycemic control actually worsened from taking sports gels to prevent hypoglycemia. When he contemplated doing an ironman distance triathlon in 2011, he sought a better method to control his diabetes. He came across the ketogenic diet in 2012 and experienced a rapid and remarkable improvement not only in glycemic control, but also in preventing hypoglycemia and its symptoms. He completed the ironman distance triathlon in 2012 without sugar, food, or hypoglycemia while in nutritional ketosis. He is now an advocate for the use of the ketogenic diet for management of diabetes and has authored books explaining its use and benefits for diabetes. He documents his results on his blog at ketogenic-diabeticathlete.wordpress.com.

Visit

www.ketogenic-diet-resource.com

for more information on ketogenic diet
research and applications, and to purchase
our other books:

*Fight Cancer with a
Ketogenic Diet*

*Conquer Type 2 Diabetes
with a Ketogenic Diet*

and Dr. Runyan's blog:

ketogenicdiabeticathlete.wordpress.com

for more information on managing type 1
diabetes.